The American Red Cross In Northern Ireland
During the Second World War

CLIVE MOORE

Published in 2023 by Northern Ireland War Memorial,
21 Talbot Street, Belfast BT1 2LD
www.niwarmemorial.org

ISBN: 978-0-9929301-8-9

The rights of Clive Moore as the author of this work have been asserted in accordance with the Copyright, Design and Patents Act 1988.

Design by John and Robyn McMillan

Printed by GPS Colour Graphics Ltd

Inside Cover
Fashion Do's and Dont's for American wives. Pamphlet produced by the American Red Cross Club Belfast, 21 June 1944.
Courtesy of Bunty Mackie Portig

Picture Credits

Every attempt has been made to trace and contact image credit holders. Credits are noted by the relevant picture. The Northern Ireland War Memorial (NIWM) and the author would like to thank the following organisations and individuals for permission to reproduce photographs in this publication: the National Archives and Records Administration (NARA), the Library of Congress, the American Red Cross, National Museums Northern Ireland (NMNI), Reading Museum, Royal Voluntary Service (RVS), the US Air Force Historical Research Agency, the Deputy Keeper of the Records at the Public Record Office of Northern Ireland (PRONI), the Belfast Telegraph, the Estate of Doris Violet Blair, Bonar Holmes, Lynne Nelson, Martin Tarr, Jon Maguire, Davy Fitzsimons, Ernie Cromie, Bunty Mackie Portig, Mary Sisson, the family of Corporal Technician Grade 5 Joseph F Mahoney and John McCann.

Second World War and World War Two

There is sometimes confusion between the terms Second World War and World War Two. The term Second World War relates to the period 3 September 1939 to 15 August 1945, while World War Two is the Americanisation which relates to a different timespan – 7 December 1941 (when America became involved in the conflict after the attack on Pearl Harbor) to 15 August 1945.

The term *Second World War* is used throughout this book as it is the term recommended by the British Commission for Military History and British publishing houses.

American Spelling

American spelling is used in this book when something specifically relates to the USA, American forces or an American organisation or is quoting an American document.

Abbreviations

8AFCC	Eighth Air Force Composite Command
AEF	American Expeditionary Force
ARC	American Red Cross
ARP	Air Raid Precautions
ATS	Auxiliary Territorial Service
CCRC	Combat Crew Replacement Centre
ENSA	Entertainments National Service Association
ETO	European Theatre of Operations
HM	His Majesty's
HQ	Headquarters
LOC	Lockheed Overseas Corporation
MOI	Ministry of Information
NAAFI	Navy Army and Air Force Institutes
NIBS	Northern Ireland Base Section
RAF	Royal Air Force
RUC	Royal Ulster Constabulary
USAAF	United States Army Air Forces
USAFBI	United States Army Forces British Isles
USANIF	United States Army Northern Ireland Force
UK	United Kingdom
US	United States
USMC	United States Marine Corps
USNOB	United States Naval Operating Base
USO	United Services Organization
WAAF	Women's Auxiliary Air Force
WVS	Women's Voluntary Services
WRNS	Women's Royal Naval Service
YMCA	Young Men's Christian Association

Foreword

A founding principle of the Northern Ireland War Memorial is the recognition of the links and friendship forged between the United States of America and Northern Ireland during the Second World War. Clive Moore has written an outstanding account of the history of the American Red Cross (ARC) in Northern Ireland that spans both World Wars. The book lays out the chronological development of this organisation which is punctuated by fascinating biographies of the key characters.

Founded by Clara Barton in Washington DC on 21 May 1881, the ARC was described in character as "giving relief to and serving as a medium of communication between members of the American armed forces and their families, as well as providing national and international relief and mitigation." The ARC was to become an intrinsic part of the United States military presence in Northern Ireland during the Second World War.

From the small beginnings of the ARC Service Club in the former Northern Counties Hotel at Waterloo Place, Derry/Londonderry opened on the 6 May 1942 and the ARC Service Club in Belfast in the Belfast Plaza opened on the 6 June 1942 to the large expansion of sites and premises that coped with the influx of US personnel into Northern Ireland prior to D-Day, ARC facilities became a common site across the country. This book is not only testament to the outstanding work of those US personnel who provided the ARC recreational services but also the organisations and people of Northern Ireland who did so much to make the US servicemen and women feel "home from home." This splendid publication shines a light on a less well-known aspect of the US military presence in Northern Ireland during the Second World War whilst at the same time giving interesting glimpses of the socio-economic history of the country during those troubled years. A must read!

D. Bigger
Chairman, Northern Ireland War Memorial

AMERICAN RED CROSS SERVICE CLUB

Acknowledgements

The author and the Council of the Northern Ireland War Memorial would like to thank: the American Red Cross, the National Archives and Records Administration, the Public Record Office of Northern Ireland, National Museums Northern Ireland, the Library of Congress, the US Air Force Historical Research Agency, the National Archives, Royal Voluntary Service, Reading Museum, and the Western Maryland Historical Library. Thanks is also expressed to the following individuals for their help, contributions, and assistance: Robert Bell, John Blair, Cathy Brown, Archie DiFante, John Duncan, Peter Cooke, Davy Fitzsimons, Alan Freeburn, Damian Gorman, Jenny Haslett, Ted Harwood, Tab Lewis, David Moore, Brian Murray, Steve Newman, Aimée Nelson, Lynne Nelson, Jim Lyttle, Jill Craig, Julie Turtle Mackie, Bunty Mackie Portig, Jon Maguire, Joe Mahoney, John McCann, Dr Leanne McCormick, John McMillan, Brian Murray, Mary O'Flynn Moore, Holly Reed, Mary Sisson, Eric Van Slander, Martin Tarr, and Susan Robbins Watson.

This publication was expertly designed by Professor John McMillan whose friendship and creativity is greatly missed by all at NIWM. The author and NIWM staff were delighted to work with his daughter, Robyn McMillan, to finish this publication and would like to thank her for her professionalism and dedication to the project.

The procurement, equipping, and maintenance of American Red Cross service clubs was carried out by the British Government as reciprocal aid. In Northern Ireland the necessary arrangements were the responsibility of the Ministry of Works and Public Buildings, who produced this illustration of standardised signage applicable to American Red Cross service clubs in January 1944.
NIWM Collection

Ernie Cromie 1942 – 2021

Lastly, this publication would not have been possible without the help and encouragement of the late Ernie Cromie (*left*). From our earliest encounters in the Sperrins and Glens of Antrim, through to weekends spent at Langford Lodge, and in more recent times, the multitude of phone calls and conversations on historical aviation matters. This book is dedicated to his memory.

Clive Moore

American Red Cross recruitment poster based on a photograph by Toni Frissell. *Library of Congress*

Contents

iv **Abbreviations**
v **Foreword**
vii **Acknowledgments**
ix **Contents**

1 **From Acorns Grow**
13 **To War Again**
36 **Evolving Needs**
52 **Aeroclubs And Clubmobiles**
62 **Expansion**
81 **The Sports Program**
93 **The Stars And Stripes War Orphans Fund**
102 **Final Days**

108 **Appendices**
113 **Sources/Bibliography**

From Acorns Grow

Although not governed by any military authority, the American Red Cross (ARC) was to become an intrinsic part of the United States (US) military presence in Northern Ireland during the Second World War. Founded by Clara Barton in Washington, DC on 21 May 1881, the organisation was described in its charter as 'giving relief to and serving as a medium of communication between members of the American armed forces and their families, as well as providing national and international disaster relief and mitigation.' From modest roots, the organisation experienced phenomenal growth after the outbreak of the First World War, with the first advance guard from the ARC sailing from New York for Europe, only 57 days after the US declaration of war.

Previously having pursued a policy of neutrality, the US entry into the war was influenced by several events. On 7 May 1915, the RMS *Lusitania* was sunk 11 miles off the southern coast of Ireland by a torpedo fired from a German U-boat. The loss of 1,198 passengers and crew, of which 123 were Americans, began a change in US public opinion. Three months later, the sinking of the New York-bound SS *Arabic* brought speculation as to whether America would enter the war and resulted in Germany abandoning its practice of unrestricted submarine warfare, albeit temporarily. The strategy was resumed in February 1917, directly contributing to the US declaration of war on 6 April 1917.

The shipping losses had demonstrated the capabilities of Germany's expanding submarine fleet and between February and April 1917, U-boats sank more than 500 merchant ships.

On 11 October 1918, twelve American victims of the Otranto *disaster were buried in Belfast City Cemetery. The photograph shows the funeral procession passing along Royal Avenue, Belfast. The wreaths were chiefly gifts of the Belfast Care Committee of the ARC.*
Library of Congress

As a countermeasure, the US Navy was deployed to bases in Ireland. First arriving in Cork on 4 May 1917, they eventually operated warships from Berehaven and Queenstown (modern day Cobh) and flying boats from five Naval Air Stations. Despite this sizeable positioning of military resources, the shipping losses continued and soon directly impacted the US military. On 5 February 1918 the troopship and former liner SS *Tuscania* was sunk by a U-boat in the North Channel between Scotland and Ireland, with over 2,000 US Army personnel on board. When official word of the sinking arrived in the US Army HQ in London, the acting disembarkation officer for Glasgow, Captain K E Rockey of the US Marine Corps (USMC) was ordered to proceed immediately to Larne in County Antrim where about 550 survivors had already been brought ashore.

The news also reached the ARC in London which offered all its available resources in Ireland and cabled the American Consul in Belfast to arrange funds and supplies. Two ARC representatives, Captain B Stuart Smith and Captain Edgar H Wells, were dispatched to Larne with the necessary resources to ensure 'that no man and no need should be overlooked.' Other Irish ports were also handling survivors. In the northwest, 75 officers and 1,274 other ranks had been landed at Londonderry and Buncrana, and were temporarily accommodated in barracks inadequate for the numbers. To relieve the situation some were transferred to camps at Randalstown, Carrickfergus and Belfast, where Smith and Wells began signing receipts for soldiers to obtain clothing and mess kits from British Army sources. Quantities of comfort supplies and tobacco were also provided, with several Americans who resided in Belfast volunteering their services to the ARC; an offer that was appreciated and increasingly necessary as the last of the recovering soldiers only left for England nearly two weeks later.

An estimated 210 lives were lost in the sinking of the *Tuscania*, and the incident displayed not only the vulnerability of shipping to U-boats, but also shortcomings in the relief effort.

Acutely aware of the potential for comparable events, the ARC promptly initiated a scheme in which a subsidiary branch of its London chapter was established in Belfast, where stores of clothing and supplies would be located at a central warehouse. A series of smaller relief depots were then established along the coast at Larne, Ballycastle, Londonderry, and Buncrana as it was felt that these were the most likely locations where survivors of any future incidents might arrive. Belfast businessman, Frederick Cleaver, was employed to oversee the relief depots and he subsequently became director of the ARC in Ireland. Sadly, the preparations proved somewhat prophetic with the plans and facilities soon tested to the full.

The Sinking of the *Otranto*

Built by the Workman Clark and Company shipyard in Belfast, the SS *Otranto* was launched in 1909 and requisitioned in 1914 by the British Admiralty. Eventually pressed into service as a troopship, the *Otranto* sailed from New York in a convoy on 25 September 1918 with 694 US Army personnel on board. From the beginning of the voyage the convoy encountered rough seas and as they neared the British Isles the weather deteriorated further. On 1 October, in the midst of a severe storm, the *Otranto* collided with another troopship, HMS *Kashmir*, just off the Scottish island of Islay. The *Kashmir* managed to continue to port however the *Otranto* lost power and drifted onto the rocky coast of Islay.

The first indications of the disaster to the wider world occurred when the destroyer HMS *Mounsey* arrived in Belfast without prior notification. Unable to communicate as its radio equipment had been damaged, the *Mounsey* manoeuvred into the dock, where a lieutenant on board called ashore, '*we've got a lot of American soldiers off the Otranto wrecked at the head of the North Channel.*'

Right. Photographed in the courtyard of Belfast City Hall, the Emergency and Hospital Committee of the Belfast branch of the ARC who had charge of relief work in Ireland after the *Otranto* disaster.
Library of Congress

Facing page. The first ARC workers to reach the scene of the *Otranto* wreck on Islay were the members of a flying squadron sent from their HQ in Belfast. The man directly in front of the flag is Lieutenant James Jeffers whose family originally came from Lurgan. Also pictured are several Belfast doctors, Captain A Davison (front row, arms folded) a New Yorker who had been connected with a Belfast shipping firm for several years, and Frederick Cleaver (centre front) who was in charge of the ARC emergency depot in Belfast.
Born in 1875, Frederick Cleaver entered the family business of Robinson & Cleaver in 1895. A few years later he was appointed as director and became chairman of the board after his father's death. Under his control the Belfast linen house prospered with Cleaver helping develop their overseas trade. In 1914, at the request of James Craig, he organised and directed the clothing and fitting out of the 36th 'Ulster' Division. He was later appointed director of the ARC in Ireland in 1917. For his service he received the American Certificate of Honor and Badge of the ARC. He died suddenly in 1936, aged 61.
Library of Congress

As the ship berthed, dialogue between ship and shore continued. A medical officer enquired about numbers and received a reply of between five and six hundred resulting in a man on the quay being ordered to, *'telephone and call through to the American Consul and tell him about these soldiers. Then get the American Red Cross. Say that we are sending the sick men to the hospitals in the city and the others to Victoria Barracks.'*

Thanks to foresight and equipment in place to respond to the unfolding events, the ARC in Belfast initiated their plans. Overseen by Fred Cleaver, packages of emergency stores were transported to Victoria Barracks and distributed among the survivors in its gymnasium. Those suffering from injuries or exposure were taken to several of Belfast's hospitals, where over the following days women from the ARC distributed 'comfort bags' of chocolate and fruit, and wrote letters for those who couldn't. More information concerning the *Otranto* incident reached Belfast and it was decided to dispatch a relief effort to Islay. Cleaver called for volunteers and an appeal was made

to the Royal Navy to provide a vessel. As a result, an ARC expedition consisting of six motor cars left Belfast that evening for Buncrana with supplies and a detail of Royal Army Medical Corps personnel. A brief stop was made in Londonderry, where a lorry filled with clothing was added to the small convoy which reached Buncrana shortly after dawn. The party then boarded a Royal Navy vessel bound for Islay, following two trawlers that had already been dispatched. Landing at Port Charlotte on Islay, it became increasingly clear that a recovery rather than a rescue operation was already underway. Having given the few survivors all assistance possible, the ARC party returned to Belfast on board a trawler after three days on the island. Meanwhile, another group of ARC personnel, among whom was Lieutenant James Jeffers, had been dispatched to Dublin from London to meet the first group of survivors who had travelled by train from Belfast for onward conveyance to England. Jeffers' involvement is noteworthy for his local connection. Born in Lurgan, County Armagh in 1882, Jeffers had emigrated to the US with his wife and settled in New Jersey. Serving in the ARC as the officer in charge of the relief, he was later commended for his actions after reaching Islay and maintained contact with the islanders long after the event.

The sinking of the *Otranto* was the worst convoy disaster of the First World War with 335 soldiers, 11 officers, and 85 crew lost in the incident. From those, 199 were buried on Islay, and a further 12 American soldiers who died from pneumonia were buried in Belfast City Cemetery. Throughout the entire operation, the ARC had provided support for the men and its establishment of the relief depots had undoubtedly saved many lives. On a visit to Belfast at the end of October, General John Biddle, commanding American troops in Great Britain and Ireland said, *'Americans owed a special debt of gratitude, for in connection with the recent terrible tragedy of the Otranto it was by Belfast that succor was given to the survivors who sick and weary were brought here.'* More broadly and beyond their relief effort in Belfast, Biddle's praise for the ARC was equally enthusiastic. Subsequently, he stated that *'We in the army all feel a gratitude to the Red Cross which it is hard for me to express in words. Without the Red Cross it would have been impossible for us to have given camps the comforts and conveniences and happiness.'*

The ARC had clearly proved its adaptability through its relief efforts in Ireland, but throughout the First World War it had primarily been tasked with service to the American armed forces, their allies, and victims of the conflict. At the conclusion of hostilities in November 1918, the ARC had become a major international humanitarian organisation with a broad and distinguished record. In the inter-war years, it withdrew its commissions and the majority of its workers from foreign service as its work overseas diminished. It also closed overseas chapters that had been formed by Americans living abroad, and focused on service to veterans, enhancing its education and training programs, and assisting in the wake of natural disasters in the US.

The Second World War

ARC involvement in the Second World War preceded the entrance of the US military into the conflict, and its activities rapidly expanded as the war escalated. During 1939 and 1940, its annual membership and fundraising drives emphasised the need for a strong response to support relief efforts in Europe. In giving help to the people of another country, the ARC worked hand in hand with existing relief organisations. In Northern Ireland, a small but significant aspect of this activity predated the arrival of US forces in 1942. Arguably it could be considered only a detail, but ARC involvement can be traced back to aid given to civilians in the aftermath of the Belfast Blitz in 1941, specifically in relation to the work carried out by the British Women's Voluntary Service (WVS). Originally founded in 1938 as the Women's Voluntary Services for Air Raid Precautions (ARP) with the intent to help recruit women into the ARP movement, the WVS was somewhat late in establishing operations in Northern Ireland. Its inaugural meeting was held in Belfast on 30 January 1941. Subsequently, both a WVS centre and the organisation's Northern Ireland HQ at Donegall Square South, Belfast opened on 3 and 12 February respectively. Appointed by the Ministry of Public Security for Northern Ireland, its president was the Duchess of Abercorn, Kathleen Hamilton, and its chairwoman was Lady Gladys Stronge, wife of Sir Norman Stronge. Indicative of the interest in their activities, the organisation had successfully enrolled 10,446 members in Northern Ireland by the end of May 1941.

At the instigation of its founder, Lady Reading, the WVS collected and distributed clothing for children, evacuees, and the homeless. In a BBC broadcast to the US, she highlighted the need for clothing within the United Kingdom (UK), and the appeal subsequently led to a number of US State Department registered organisations such as Bundles for Britain, the British War Relief Society, and the ARC, sending quantities of donated clothing to the UK, which were distributed from WVS emergency clothing stores. As wartime events evolved during 1941, the establishment of the WVS within Northern Ireland was timely. Like other UK cities, Belfast came to the attention of the Luftwaffe's bombing campaign. It was subjected to four air raids which between them saw the loss of over 900 lives. Fortuitously, the first shipment of ARC clothing reached Northern Ireland on 20 April 1941: only four days after the second and largest raid on Easter Tuesday.

An ARC poster from 1941 promoting the War Relief campaign. The poster was widely distributed throughout the US, and it stimulated financial and public support for the War Relief Fund. *American Red Cross*

Junction of York Street and Donegall Street, Belfast after an air raid in 1941.
PRONI CAB/3/A/131

The Welfare Branch of the Health Division tasked with assisting the public following an enemy attack recorded that the WVS had received 112,500 articles of clothing, 12,000 blankets, as well as numerous culinary or table utensils and £100 in cash from the ARC. Northern Ireland went on to receive approximately 20 tons of donations from 87 ARC chapters from across the US. To assess exactly how WVS operations in Northern Ireland were making use of the clothing supplied, the ARC Director for Civilian War Relief in Western Europe, Mr William H Giblin arrived from London on 16 June for a five-day fact-finding tour. Giblin visited four counties and conducted over 50 interviews which included among them: the US Consul General, local civil servants, military personnel, and numerous members of the WVS.

William H Giblin, ARC Director for Civilian War Relief in Western Europe, photographed in October 1941. Giblin visited Northern Ireland in June of that year to assess the use of ARC clothing donations and mobile canteen operations.
Courtesy of The American Red Cross. All Rights Reserved in all countries.
© *The American National Red Cross 1941. 13009-001*

In his subsequent report Giblin noted that the ARC clothing was particularly valuable both after the Easter Tuesday Raid, then during and immediately following the Fire Raid in May. He observed that one district alone had clothed 800 people, and overall, he was most impressed by the WVS operations within Northern Ireland, describing the regional clothing depot as 'very efficient and from an ARC viewpoint well worth visiting.' Only one aspect of WVS and ARC co-operation raised a minor concern and that was the marking of ARC sponsored vehicles.

In 1939 the WVS began to recruit volunteers to work in mobile canteens, which were primarily used to feed Civil Defence workers and civilians wherever the need might arise. Essentially these were small vans fitted out to provide refreshments and light snacks, and many were financed by sources in the US. By 1941, four such vehicles, with another still to be delivered were funded by the ARC and stationed at Wandsworth House in Belfast. Each canteen was to be appropriately marked indicating its association with the ARC, but only one carried any reference and the application of that wasn't viewed as being appropriate. However, Giblin was judicious in his perception of the situation and concluded it was, 'due to a careless mistake on the part of the builders of the canteen and no fault of the local people.' He also recommended that the region would benefit from a fifth mobile canteen in addition to the one already on order.

A mobile canteen funded by the ARC in use in England during 1941 and operated by the WVS. Five similar WVS vehicles were used in Northern Ireland and also funded through the ARC. *Copyright Reading Museum (Reading Borough Council) All rights reserved*

Clothing donations and mobile canteens raised awareness of the ARC in Northern Ireland before the official arrival of US forces in January 1942. Giblin emphasised that 'the American Red Cross gifts to Great Britain were a practical manifestation of the interest and sympathy of the American people for the people of Britain.' Unknown to all including Giblin, just over seven months later the same ARC funded canteen vehicles he had observed in Belfast were to be employed by the WVS in the provision of refreshments to the first US troops arriving in Northern Ireland. However, it was some months before the ARC secured its own substantial presence in Northern Ireland to support American military operations, most prominently in the form of its service clubs.

To War Again

Formal representation by the ARC in the UK during the Second World War began just over three months before America's entry into the conflict when the American National Red Cross Committee in Great Britain was established. Headed by the American Ambassador to Great Britain, John G Winant, the committee mainly comprised of American businessmen based in London. Significantly, during October 1941 they were joined by ARC staff member Bernard S Carter, who arrived from Washington, DC, after previously finishing an assignment in Paris. Carter took up the position of the ARC delegate to the British Isles and his appointment to the role would soon influence ARC operations throughout the region, directly contributing to the creation of the first two ARC service clubs in Northern Ireland.

Only days after the arrival of the first US troops in Belfast in January 1942, the ARC Welfare & Recreation Services in London received a communication from Major General James E Chaney, commanding US Army Forces in the British Isles (USAFBI), informing them that the ARC was now designated as the sole welfare agency to work with troops under his command. That communication was also relayed to Chief of Staff General Marshall, who implemented it as an order affecting all the American military theatres of operations. However, Marshall's orders amended Chaney's by not only stating that the US Army would be responsible for its own welfare and recreation, but that the ARC could take these over when military or other

Facing page
The SS *Duchess of Atholl* arriving in Belfast on 2 March 1942. Among the personnel onboard was the first small contingent of ARC staff.
Author's Collection

requirements made it desirable. This last factor and its relevance to the UK was pressed by Carter during February 1942 in a cable from London to the ARC Chairman in Washington, DC, Norman Davis. In his message, Carter pointed out that it was impractical for the army to operate clubs outside troop areas, and perhaps more pertinently, Carter felt soldiers also enjoyed the change of atmosphere offered by an establishment run by non-military personnel. Meanwhile, Colonel J E Dahlquist at HQ USAFBI instructed Carter to proceed immediately with the establishment of service clubs in both Belfast and Londonderry. Accordingly, Carter requested the initial funding requirement which was approved by General Chaney on 22 February. In parallel, the establishment of suitable sites in London was also initiated.

Photographed in New York staff who arrived in Northern Ireland on 2 March with the second contingent of US troops. *Author's Collection*

The next advancement in Northern Ireland occurred when ARC representative, Robert C Lewis arrived and began making arrangements. He wrote to Carter outlining proposals for taking over both the Ulster Hall in Belfast and the Northern Counties Hotel in Londonderry, but only the latter would come to fruition. Possibly by design rather than chance, his visit coincided with the arrival of the first group of ARC personnel to Northern Ireland, who had travelled across the Atlantic with the second contingent of American troops that disembarked in Belfast on 2 March.

Preparations for their departure from the US encountered a few unforeseen issues, as exactly who would be travelling had yet to be finalised. Initially, a group of five was scheduled to depart with the first contingent of troops in January, but through lack of available space, they were forced to remain behind. From that initial selection, two personnel were then substituted for two others, requiring swift approval from the US War Department's Provost Marshall's Investigations Division. The group was then doubled from five to ten staff only days before the sailing, necessitating the army to rapidly select a corresponding number of its personnel to leave behind. Eventually, on 19 February the group departed from New York, sailing on board the SS *Duchess of Atholl* with troops from the 34th Infantry Division. Most significantly, within the group was the man appointed as regional field director for the ARC in Northern Ireland, Mr John S Disosway, and recreation director, Thomas Irving from Rockford, Illinois who would soon be instrumental in establishing the ARC club in Belfast. To administer their operations in Northern Ireland, the group established its HQ in an allocated Nissen hut within the grounds of Wilmont House, which was already HQ for United States Army Northern Ireland Force (USANIF).

Among the ARC personnel in this first contingent were four medical social workers assigned to the 5th General Hospital at Musgrave Park, Belfast and 10th Station Hospital at Ebrington Barracks, Londonderry.

Arranging welfare for their American patients, these four women were the first ARC staff in Northern Ireland fulfilling the organisation's intended role for the military. For the others, their task included preparing for the eventual opening of service clubs and consequently, further groups of ARC personnel arrived via England over the following weeks. But even with increasing staff numbers, it would still be over a month before any actual premises were ready for use as a service club. In the interim, further properties were viewed for potential suitability, and the necessary steps were then taken to secure and prepare them. As the first of the clubs neared completion, awareness of their coming was raised by the military through the inaugural UK edition of *Stars and Stripes* newspaper, which informed its readers that:

'*The first Red Cross recreation centers for American forces in Northern Ireland will be opened within 60 days, J. S. Disosway, Field Director, has announced. Two centers, one in Belfast and the other at Londonderry, will be among the first ready to receive soldiers. These will be located in buildings already available and will provide rooms, showers, and meals for soldiers. Present plans indicate that a charge of half a crown will be made for one night's lodging, a shower, and breakfast. Soldiers on pass or furlough will be admitted to these and other recreation centers to be opened within the next several months.*'

A Little Bit of America

Although the ARC had been involved in providing services at the American Eagle Club in London a fortnight earlier, the first dedicated ARC service club in the UK opened on 6 May 1942 in the former Northern Counties Hotel at Waterloo Place, Londonderry. Work began on the club several weeks earlier with a small army of workmen preparing the premises and carrying out necessary alterations. At the club's formal opening ceremony, guests included Bernard Carter, and the two most senior officers from the US military then stationed in Northern Ireland, Captain William J Larson, Commanding Officer of the United States Naval Operating Base Londonderry (USNOB), and Major General Russell P Hartle, Commander of USANIF. Appointed as the club's staff were Club Director, Frank R Goodall, Assistant Club Director, Mrs Eleanor Kohler, and Program Director, Alfred Cappio. The opening generated considerable interest in the local press with headlines such as, 'A little bit of America' and 'Hot Dogs and Hamburgers for Troops.' Added to which were observations on cultural differences for the curious, with one newspaper noting that American shower rooms had been installed, as the organiser believed, 'that the American boys will prefer showers to the use of tub baths over here.'

Bernard S Carter, ARC Delegate to the British Isles, photographed during the opening of the first ARC club in the UK at the former Northern Counties Hotel in Londonderry. On the left is Lady Sinclair from the ARC, and Captain William J Larson, Commanding Officer of the USNOB Londonderry. On the right is Major General Russell P Hartle, Commander of USANIF.
Author's Collection

The Londonderry service club effectively provided a model for subsequent ARC facilities, and their records noted that much of the organisation's pioneering work in recreational activity and athletics in the European Theatre of Operations (ETO) originated there. Its entertainment and sports programmes gave the club a high degree of popularity, but its establishment was not without teething troubles. One particular issue was brought to the attention of Bernard Carter on 27 May at a meeting with Sir Harold Boulton from the British Foreign Office. Boulton had recently visited Londonderry and recounted a situation that Robert Lewis had described as follows, 'the British were monopolizing our club in Derry, and as a result, the American sailors and soldiers were disgruntled and felt that they were being crowded out of their own club.' Seeking a resolution, Boulton arranged for a meeting to take place between the ARC and the three British services, recommending that Lewis attend. In preparation and ahead of his flight from London, Lewis held a meeting at the US embassy in London, with Captains Larson and Davis from the USNOB. Before that, both men had spoken with Boulton, voicing the collective feeling that a 'certain curtailment by the British was essential.' However, Larson and Davis were adamant that the British should not be excluded completely.

American soldiers, sailors and a Women's Auxiliary Air Force (WAAF) member relaxing in the lounge of the Londonderry ARC club shortly after its opening in May 1942. *Author's Collection*

The meeting was held at the office of the Royal Navy Commodore Ross Stewart and attended by delegates from the three British services. Representing the interests of the ARC with Robert Lewis was Frank Goodall. In his following report, Lewis felt the meeting went well and was pleased with how it was conducted and the attitude of the officers present. Elaborating, Lewis said a number of points had been established to clarify the relationship between the ARC club, its use by British personnel, and how to reach a mutually favourable arrangement. Essentially, access for British personnel would become more controlled, particularly at weekends, and a weekly direct communication was opened between the Londonderry ARC Club Director and the Royal Navy base every Friday. It would then be the responsibility of the relevant British officer to issue the necessary stamped passes for any available spaces. It was also to be made clear to all ranks that the ARC reserved the right to control the facilities available in the club to British personnel, and that numbers were sometimes restricted to protect their main objective: the welfare of American personnel.

Eventually, ARC protocol dictated that within their service clubs, members of the British forces were welcome as the guests of American personnel, but otherwise, they did not have access to ARC club facilities. Accordingly, it was felt only fair that American troops should not use British facilities, such as Navy, Army, and Air Force Institutes (NAAFI) and Young Men's Christian Association (YMCA) canteens. Naturally, there were a few exceptions to the rule, such as the Officers' Club located on High Street, Belfast which provided a full range of facilities aside from sleeping accommodation. This particular venue had existed before the activation of the ARC clubs and membership was open to commissioned officers from all the allied forces, including those from the women's services. Unusually, family members were also permitted entry as guests. Later in the war, examples of other establishments included the Lion & Eagle Club on William Street, Londonderry, which opened on

1 September 1943, and provided service for both British and American personnel. Later, but on a much smaller scale, the NAAFI in Newry was singled out as an example of a special case suitable for both British and American use.

One existing example of a facility providing welfare for military personnel was the Officers' Club on High Street, Belfast. Dances were held every Friday and Saturday evening from 9pm to 1am and the facilities were used by some ARC staff members. *NARA*

A selection of the food available at the Lion & Eagle Club in Londonderry. It opened in September 1943 on William Street and was intended to foster better relations between American and British personnel. *NARA*

Mutual Interests

The clarification and resolution of admittance procedures was timely as ARC plans and facilities within Northern Ireland were evolving and expanding in the wake of increasing American troop arrivals and movements. Alongside some staffing and administration changes, the most significant occurrence was the tentative opening of the largest ARC service club in Northern Ireland, which was in the former Plaza Ballroom on Chichester Street, Belfast. The need for organised social facilities for American personnel in the city was recognised immediately after their arrival. On 31 January, the *Northern Whig* reported under the headline 'Ulster-American Hostesses', that several American women living in Northern Ireland were planning to entertain the American troops, having been in touch with their units and helping with shopping tours and in other ways. Somewhat prophetically, the newspaper also reported that 'They are at present negotiating for club rooms in which it will be possible to offer entertainment on seven days a week and under an American hostess.' Notably the article cited Mrs Victor Cooke (Alice) and Mrs J A Mackie (Marcia) as being instrumental in providing the services. Both would become key employees of the Belfast ARC service club. The two women had more in common than a passing interest in providing hospitality for service personnel. Both were American citizens, both lived in Greenisland and both had married men from Northern Ireland.

Marcia Mackie
Courtesy of Bunty Mackie Portig

BIOGRAPHY: MARCIA MACKIE

Marcia Mackie's involvement with the ARC was as fortuitous as it was inevitable. Born in Boston, Massachusetts in 1905 and educated at The Winsor School and Vassar College, Marcia Mackie arrived in Northern Ireland through her marriage to James Mackie of James Mackie & Sons Ltd, who operated a foundry on the Springfield Road, Belfast. Living at Meroc House in Greenisland with their four children, their home became a frequent venue for entertaining James Mackie's business friends, as well as an impromptu social centre for the comparatively large group of Americans then living in Northern Ireland.

Life was not restricted to Meroc and her other activities somewhat pointed towards the qualities she would employ in her eventual wartime role. When the Royal Maternity Hospital Ladies' Guild was formed in 1935, Marcia became the honorary secretary and later rose to the position of vice-president by the end of 1940. The war soon started to influence Marcia's endeavours and in her role as honorary secretary of the Ulster Hospitals' Library Service, an appeal was made for books suitable for seamen recovering in hospitals from injuries sustained in the Atlantic. With neighbour and compatriot Alice Cooke, she became involved with the Allied Seamen's Hospitality Committee on its American sub-committee and then with the assistance of Mrs Malcolm Gordon, formed the Ulster American Hospitality Committee early in 1942.

The exact point at which Marcia became a member of the ARC staff is unclear but by November 1942 she was serving in the role of assistant director of the Belfast ARC service club. Similarly, when she became its director is again unknown, but evidence exists of her having achieved that position by April 1943, making her the first female director of an ARC service club outside of the US. The role would require her qualities as administrator, hostess, and counsellor.

Sleeve patch
belonging to Mackie
Courtesy of Bunty Mackie Portig

For her work with the ARC, Marcia was awarded an OBE in June 1945 and presented with the American Medal of Freedom during a reception at the Grand Central Hotel in 1948. When the Northern Ireland Hospitals Authority came into being in 1948, Marcia's considerable experience within welfare and health care made her a natural choice for membership. She became the vice chairwoman from 1956, then from 1965-67 its chairwoman, receiving a CBE for her services. In 1968 she received an honorary Doctorate of Laws (LLD) from Queen's University Belfast and the following year accepted an

ARC Zone Director Herbert E Knude, with ARC Secretary Patricia Stevenson and Marcia Mackie on Montgomery Street, Belfast. *Courtesy of Bunty Mackie Portig*

appointment to the Senate of the University. Although Marcia Mackie passed away in March 1973, her name continues in the contribution of welfare to others through the Royal College of Nursing Foundation's Marcia Mackie Bursary Scheme, which offers financial support to registered nurses in Northern Ireland who wish to enhance nursing through personal professional development.

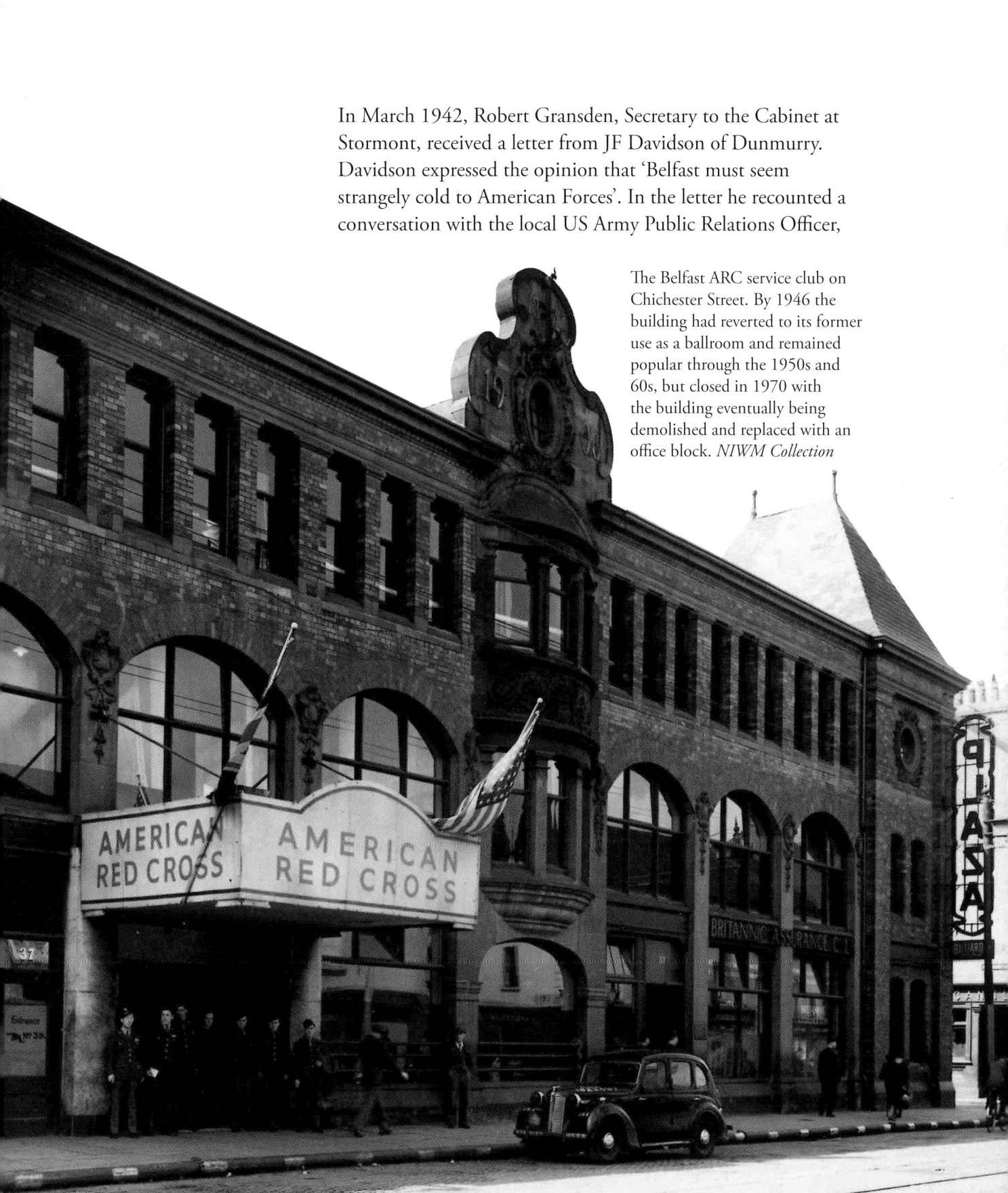

In March 1942, Robert Gransden, Secretary to the Cabinet at Stormont, received a letter from JF Davidson of Dunmurry. Davidson expressed the opinion that 'Belfast must seem strangely cold to American Forces'. In the letter he recounted a conversation with the local US Army Public Relations Officer,

The Belfast ARC service club on Chichester Street. By 1946 the building had reverted to its former use as a ballroom and remained popular through the 1950s and 60s, but closed in 1970 with the building eventually being demolished and replaced with an office block. *NIWM Collection*

Colonel Theodore Arter, who said that men coming to Belfast on leave were a serious problem, elaborating, 'They tried to limit the passes, but even so a number filtered in, and the job was to prevent the men from getting into bad company or spending their time drinking in hotel rooms.' Davidson felt that if a large hotel or house could be taken over and converted for use as a social centre, 'Ulster's prestige would be greatly enhanced in the eyes of the American Public.' Unknown to Davidson, plans for such a facility were already well underway.

The site and building that eventually became the Belfast ARC service club began its life as the premises for Robson's Mart and Royal Victoria Horse Bazaar. Founded in 1842, the property was substantially rebuilt around 1906, but by 1930 had found a new use as a dance hall. Under the alias of Belfast Plaza's *Palais de Danse*, the building was severely damaged by fire in April 1940, leaving a shell to which some refurbishment work had already taken place by 1942. News of its impending use by the ARC was reported in Belfast's newspapers on 7 April. The largely similar articles reported that negotiations were in progress for acquiring the Belfast Plaza 'with a view to repairing the premises and establishing a United States Welfare Centre under the American Red Cross.' They further explained that it would be a combined hostel, social centre, and restaurant for American troops on leave, with the possibility of further premises being taken for use as dormitories and recreation rooms also suggested.

Described in *Stars and Stripes* as having been 'Belfast's swankiest dance hall and amusement center', the ARC had been given priority to acquire the venue. Initial plans envisaged the use of only two rooms, but throughout the building's ongoing refurbishment, evolving and escalating requirements led to sizeable expansion. Local Ministry of Finance technical officers helped with construction, adaptation, and maintenance, and it was noted they seemed to carry out their work with greater speed than for similar departments. The club's main hall was rebuilt similarly to the previous dance hall, but was now more austere in appearance. The remainder of the building retained much of its earlier form so that the premises might be returned to its previous purpose with ease. As the most prominent ARC club location in Northern Ireland, the range of facilities available when completed were extensive. The first point of call was often the information counter where cables could be sent under the direction of Alice Cooke. While the other principal staff at the time of its opening were Club Director, Thomas Irving, Assistant Club Director, Louisa Farrand and Program Director, Edwin Martin. Undoubtedly the focal point of the club was the main hall. During the day it was frequently used for sports such as boxing and basketball, but in the evening it was transformed into a dance hall. The club also included more mundane but no less essential facilities such as a lounge, library, games room, cloakrooms, a barber's shop, a shoeshine bar, canteen, and a dining room that only closed between 2:30 am and 4:30 am.

Photographed in 1931, the American Consulate in Belfast on the corner of Adelaide Street and Donegall Square South also provided additional ARC dormitory accommodation for American personnel. The building was demolished after the war and the site is now an office block presently occupied by the Bank of Ireland.
NMNI BELUM.Y3039 ©Ulster Museum Collection

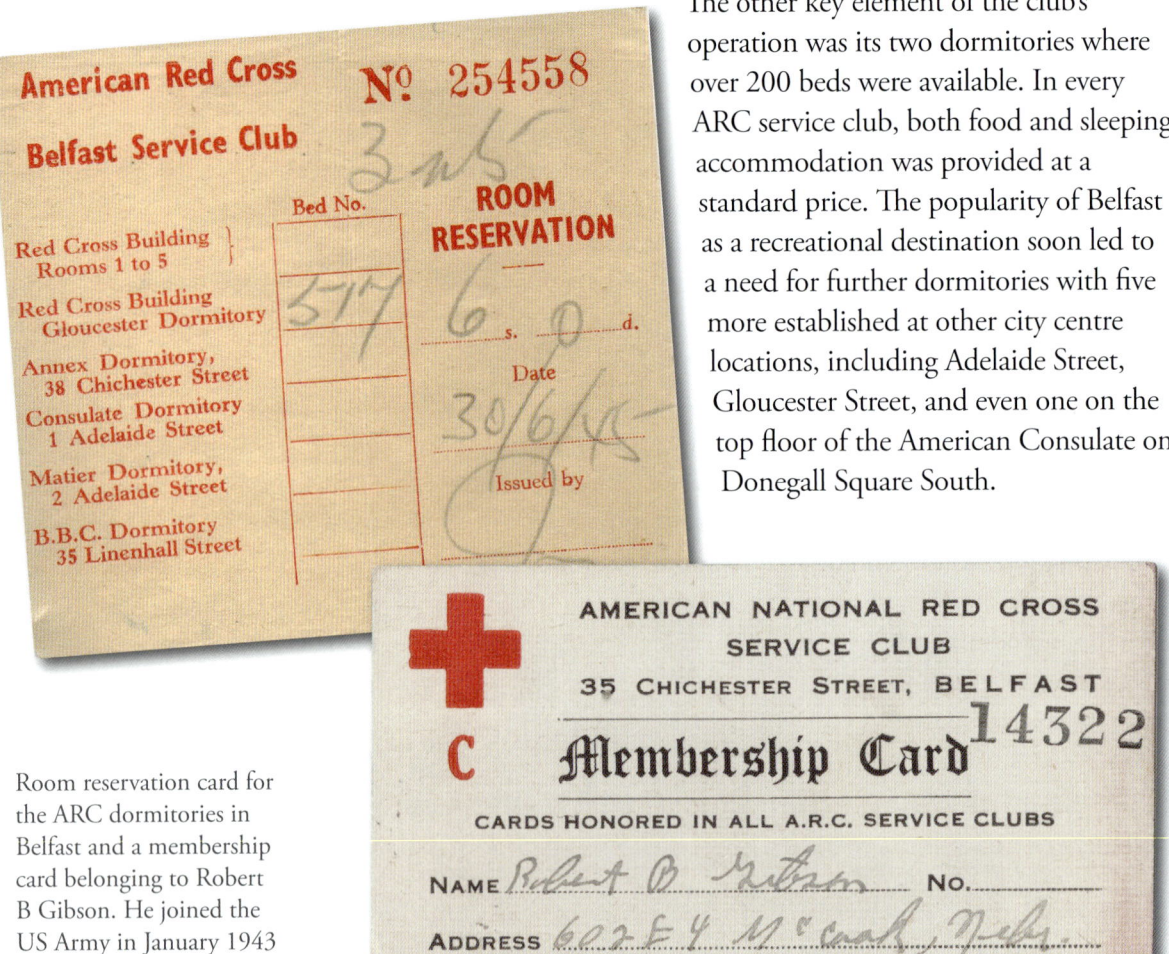

The other key element of the club's operation was its two dormitories where over 200 beds were available. In every ARC service club, both food and sleeping accommodation was provided at a standard price. The popularity of Belfast as a recreational destination soon led to a need for further dormitories with five more established at other city centre locations, including Adelaide Street, Gloucester Street, and even one on the top floor of the American Consulate on Donegall Square South.

Room reservation card for the ARC dormitories in Belfast and a membership card belonging to Robert B Gibson. He joined the US Army in January 1943 and arrived in Northern Ireland in October 1943, being assigned to Base Censor Office No.1 in Belfast. *Davy Fitzsimons and Author's collection*

In addition, two ARC hostels specifically for officers were opened. One was located at the Kensington Hotel in College Square, and the other at the Union Hotel on Donegall Square South. Both provided full facilities for American officers. At its peak, the Belfast ARC club employed 185 staff who were assisted by 450 volunteers, of which 17 were American civilian women who lived in Belfast.

Teething Troubles

Initially, the club's resources and facilities were limited as refurbishment of the premises was still ongoing. The pressing need for an ARC service club in Belfast meant that it had been decided early during reconstruction to open as soon as possible, regardless of the inconvenience to staff or the inadequate space for an activity program. Club Director Thomas W Irving stated, 'It was a very difficult situation to begin with, as we were still painting, decorating and doing minor alterations.'

As a result, on 6 June 1942, the club began business with no ceremony, no heat, no running water, and without a proper canteen or method of providing breakfast for any of the men staying overnight. At first, an ad hoc canteen comprising of three smoky *Primus* stoves was set up. Food was served at the information counter and water carried back and forth from the men's lavatory.

Pictured in the canteen of the Belfast ARC club, Canteen Supervisor, Mildred Hughes, and Mrs Curran, a local volunteer. Mildred Hughes was one of several American nationals working in the ARC club who arrived in Northern Ireland through marriage. Her husband Samuel J Hughes was head of the Colonial Department of William Ewart & Son Ltd, a notable linen manufacturer. *NARA*

An ARC volunteer's indoor uniform, previously worn by a member of the staff in Belfast. A long-sleeved one-piece garment made from poplin fabric, which was worn by all qualified volunteers and qualified paid staff. The coloured epaulets indicated roles (such as red for administration and blue for canteen staff) while paid staff and non-enrolled volunteers wore plain epaulets. Appropriate sleeve insignia was also worn. *NIWM Collection*

After ten days of cooking in this way, a more appropriate four-burner gas range arrived and by July an average of 300 men a day and up to 2,000 at the weekends were being served food. Canteen Supervisor, Mrs Mildred Hughes, was another American living in Belfast. The menu was limited due to the compact space, but it was still capable of providing a good breakfast, or lunches and sandwiches, with army rations of beef and other meats. A few popular American brands such as *Coca-Cola* and *Nabisco* were also available and the introduction of coffee, hot buttered toast, milk, and doughnuts was heartily approved of by the clientele.

The kitchen arrangement wasn't the only area of the club in need of refinement. The only place for entertainment was the recreation room that was dominated by a table tennis table acquired from the SS *Queen of Bermuda* which was requisitioned for Admiralty use and put into Belfast in 1939. Other scavenged items included a billiard table bought at auction, a piano, a dartboard, radio, lounge chairs, books, magazines, newspapers, table games, and a selection of musical instruments which provided a more comprehensive range of recreational activities.

The musical instruments became less popular after the arrival of a *Victrola* radio-gramophone complete with 108 records, which won immediate favour with visiting personnel, although the popularity of the records drowned out the men who enjoyed playing the piano. Program Director Edwin Martin recalled, 'As the club never closes the records are played until three or four o'clock on many mornings and when the bed accommodation is exhausted some boys sit up all night listening to music, their only complaints being the lack of records by Bing Crosby, Ink Spots, Jimmie Lunceford and those from the Red Seal label.' Assistant Club Director Louisa Farrand added that 'So many requests were made that they were soon purchased locally and played constantly.'

Still in the process of finding its feet, the club began to tentatively organise an entertainment programme with some mixed results.

After a meeting with the commanding officers from the Auxiliary Territorial Service (ATS), Women's Royal Naval Service (WRNS), and Women's Auxiliary Air Force (WAAF) Northern Ireland, some 500 female British military personnel received invitations to a large dance held on 10 June 1942 in the Ulster Hall. Free soda water and cakes were served for refreshments, with the music provided by a US Army orchestra, supplemented during the intermission by a local Belfast singer, Anna Meakin. The male to female ratio may have proved agreeable to the men but for the women the opposite was true. Seemingly the dance had not been sufficiently advertised among the American forces and only a limited number of men were present. However, the ARC felt that 'when we are in our own quarters the problem will reverse itself and we will have difficulty in obtaining enough girls.' Teething troubles persisted into July when Captain Doc Smith's Hill Billy Band performed to only ten people, and a lecture by a Mr Storey with accompanying lantern slides of

ARC Field Director Ford. McHale, ARC Secretary Marjorie Stein, and Zone Director Herbert E Knude at Northern Ireland's ARC Regional HQ within the grounds of Wilmont House, October 1942. *NARA*

Northern Ireland was attended by 20 people. The discouraging attendance at both was attributed to some 'glorious weather and a desire on the part of the boys to walk the streets and see Belfast.' The club had been functioning for nearly a month before a small opening ceremony was held on Saturday 4 July 1942 to coincide with American Independence Day and it was attended by the Duchess of Abercorn. That following Sunday, the chaplain for Northern Ireland Base Command, Major William T Brundick, conducted an Independence Day service from the ARC HQ at Wilmont House which was transcribed for broadcast to the US.

Meanwhile in Londonderry, the ARC club had also begun to firmly establish itself with a notable increase in the bed, bath, and breakfast services provided. During July, 1,310 men were accommodated against the previous month's total of 369, and demand began to outstrip its capacity with delays in the laundering of bed linen hindering full bed usage. As with Belfast, hiccups in running the club and discovering limitations were all part of the learning curve. The demand for showers was greater than the supply of hot water, even after the installation of two gas heaters. Water use then exceeded the capacity of the intake pipes from the city's mains supply, requiring contracts being let for a larger connection and an increased storage tank.

Embarrassingly, plumbing problems persisted when the toilet facilities proved inadequate when operating at peak capacity. Another ongoing problem was the provision of movies with equipment compatibility, related logistical issues, and the availability of a shared generator culminating in an almost complete collapse of the bi-weekly cinema programme. However, the Royal Navy came to the rescue by opening its Sunday afternoon and evening shows to American personnel as a stopgap measure.

For every setback, there was equal measured progress. During July, 90 scheduled events were held with a conservative estimate at just under 5,000 men participating. The services' league featuring athletic games and contests involved twelve US Army, Navy, and Marine teams, two Royal Air Force (RAF) teams, and two British Army teams. Matches were arranged in baseball, ping-pong, tennis, billiards, badminton, and softball. For the latter, a demonstration game was held for the benefit of British personnel where the game was thoroughly explained, and a further participation game was scheduled. To reciprocate, the British were to stage a similar event demonstrating cricket. Regular Sunday sightseeing tours were arranged when available transport permitted. Beginning at 9:30am, a bus carrying 35 people left the club and visited sites along the north coast such as Portrush, Ballintoy, and of course the Giant's Causeway – a tour that became a staple part of ARC activities.

Assistant Club Director Elena Kohler (right) at the reception desk of the Londonderry service club. Widowed in 1940, Kohler had previously worked in Switzerland with the League of Nations American Association and was motivated to join the ARC after feeling that her husband would have also contributed to the war effort. She departed New York on 22 April 1942 and was assigned as Assistant Club Director for the Londonderry ARC club. In recognition of her service with the ARC, she attended a function at Buckingham Palace on 26 November and soon after was re-assigned to North Africa, arriving in Algiers on Christmas Eve 1942. *Author's Collection*

Dances were organised as often as bands and orchestras were available. An early event featured the first appearance from the 14-piece band from the 135th Infantry Regiment named 'Ambassadors of Swing'. For these larger events, Kohler organised for women to attend, but for smaller informal tea dances held on Sundays, the men were permitted to bring their own dates. From the canteen, *Coca-Cola* was the favourite beverage with coffee second. Hot dogs proved popular and were easy to cook, but hamburgers did not prove to be as successful, often being cold and overdone when served. With the variety and type of food considered unacceptable, it was felt that a change in the canteen was needed, and after a considerable search, a young woman from Omagh was recruited.

Coming from a family-run hotel background, with three years of training at a domestic science college, Olive McIlveen was described as quietly competent, having a charming personality, and being ultimately 'splendid and just what is needed.' Two weeks after her arrival there was a noticeable improvement in canteen food, variety in menus, and general cleanliness of the kitchen. The canteen itself was soon enlarged to twice its size. After an upturn in visitor numbers in August, negotiations began for further dormitory premises nearby.

Goodall considered the problems in Londonderry as being 'somewhat unique,' largely due to it being a naval base, but also a day leave town for army personnel. The club experienced a transient clientele illustrated by the movement of troops away from camps in the surrounding area, temporarily curtailing many arranged activities and reducing the number of spectators and participants.

Evolving Needs

The opening of further ARC premises in Northern Ireland mirrored the locations where American troops were deployed. County Down, in particular, saw a more localised requirement for ARC services after the 1st Armored Division established its HQ at Castlewellan Castle, with its associated units dispersed in the surrounding countryside. The process for assessing where ARC clubs would be located was determined by both the US

Private First Class Richard Eagle and Sergeant Robert Minard in the home of a local family, showing them their American gas mask. Home hospitality visits were first organised during late 1942 but it was not until a year later that they achieved the level of success first envisaged. *Library of Congress*

military and the ARC, beginning with a survey to locate suitable buildings such as hotels, clubs, or halls. This was followed by the premises being requisitioned or rented by the Ministry of Finance (as agents for HM Commissioners of Works and Public Buildings) for the ARC. Under the reverse Lend-Lease scheme, the properties were then leased by the Crown and no rental charges were made against the ARC. In Castlewellan, a Mr Adams, who was the appointed ARC recreational worker for the 1st Armored Division, surveyed the area and found that suitable space was available in the town free of rent. Furthermore, an existing committee had previously been providing for British troops stationed in the area before their departure. With premises and the necessary organised community support already in place, Adams submitted a proposal which was approved by Robert Lewis, with the understanding that the club would be operated under the direct supervision of the ARC. Further clubs were also opened at Mourne Park and Downpatrick, where 100 ATS personnel were promptly invited to attend a dance on 20 August 1942.

To develop harmonious relationships between locals and Americans, the British Foreign Office established a committee in May 1942 to deal with hospitality for American forces in the British Isles. After a visit to Northern Ireland by the committee's acting liaison officer, Sir Harold Boulton, interest in participation within that committee was voiced by Stormont. Their feeling was that 'the [local] Government as such should not be completely ignored in the planning of hospitality arrangements for the American forces in Northern Ireland.' However, the view in London was that the constitution of the existing committee was such that it was not desirable to have any further representation on it. Moreover, London was trying to correlate American hospitality through the Ministry of Information (MOI) but in the future, Boulton would consult with Stormont, or any other organisations interested, when dealing with welfare problems in the country. At the beginning of August, a representative from the MOI's Regional Office met with Louisa Farrand, who'd been assigned the responsibility for the ARC home hospitality section in Northern Ireland. At the meeting, it was decided that Farrand should first contact General Hartle to establish if the US Army was to be in charge of the scheme, or whether the ARC should undertake its organisation with the help of other bodies.

With a preference for the last option, Farrand met the Minister of Commerce, Sir Basil Brooke, on 28 August and discussed questions of hospitality over lunch. Brooke thought it would be quite easy to arrange this with the various women's organisations and the ARC, telling her that the main consideration was to maintain good relations. But efforts to provide those were questioned in London. At their HQ, some ARC staff were becoming increasingly concerned that the WVS was trying to get a foothold in their burgeoning welfare programme. In a letter to Washington, DC, citing the actions of Lady Reading, ARC delegate to Great Britain William E Stevenson, wrote about his concern that Reading was 'bringing pressure to bear from every angle to accomplish this end.' Additionally, the hospitality programme was also met with some criticism from Stevenson, describing how the British had become stirred up about the importance of setting aside their traditional reserve, and doing everything possible to welcome Americans, noting that the press, organisations, and individuals were all urging the British to open their homes. Stevenson took the view that the British had been hospitable enough as it was and that all the talk and propaganda had been based on an exaggerated idea of the need. He also felt that the desire of the American soldier to do as he pleases when on leave had been overlooked. However, the scheme had prominent support from Lieutenant General Eisenhower, a fact that Stevenson felt had not gone unnoticed by Lady Reading. To what extent any similar concerns were duplicated in Belfast would be conjecture, but after the meeting with Farrand, Brooke recorded that he felt she was an 'alarmist and some of her remarks were right off the point.' At another meeting with Brigadier General Edmund Hill from the United

States Army Air Forces (USAAF) and Lady Stronge from the WVS, the arrangement of hospitality for the junior officers of the US Army was discussed. The concerted view was that they were 'rather lost and very often go about with the wrong people.' At the meeting's conclusion, Brooke surmised that 'I think we fixed it by cutting out a good deal of the Red Cross interference.'

Photographed outside the Guildhall in Londonderry is Lady Reading (standing front centre), with members of the ARC and Lieutenant Colonel Leonard R Greenfield (second from right), Commanding Officer, 1st Battalion, 133rd Infantry Regiment, 34th Infantry Division, US Army.
Royal Voluntary Service WRVS/HQ/P/PER/LR018

By September 1942, Stormont had begun organising a hospitality committee with its own broader remit 'to deal comprehensively with questions affecting the welfare of all the fighting services, both British and American.' The heads of the services, including General Hartle, were invited to serve on the committee together with representatives from any of the government departments directly affected. Chaired by Brooke, the first meeting of what was now called the Northern Ireland Troop Welfare Committee was held at Belfast Castle on Thursday 10 September. At the meeting were seven representatives from the British forces, three members of local government, the RUC inspector–general, and two members of the American forces, Colonel Haley, US Army and Lieutenant Commander Sperry, US Navy. After Brooke's opening statement and aside from discussion on Sunday openings for cinemas, alcohol, and other questions which Brooke felt the civil departments could adequately deal with, the matter of private hospitality for the forces was raised. Brooke outlined the proposal to set up a hospitality committee comprised of various interested organisations in Northern Ireland. Their task was to submit to the ARC and the welfare officers of the British fighting services, approved lists of suitable hosts who would be prepared to provide private hospitality to members of the Allied forces in Northern Ireland. No representatives from either the

Personnel from USAAF Station 236 Toome enjoying home hospitality with the Shipway family. *Courtesy of Lynne Nelson*

ARC or WVS were invited to the meeting, which was also an entirely male affair. Subsequently, it was another six days before Brooke recorded that he had decided to ask Lady Stronge from the WVS to run the hospitality committee.

Entrusted with organising private hospitality for American and British forces, Lady Stronge convened a series of meetings throughout Northern Ireland and with the assistance of the MOI regional information officer, 15 committees were established in larger towns. The first were formed in Lurgan and Lisburn on 12 October with Belfast's committee forming on 17 December. A further four were established in January 1943, the last of which was in Banbridge. These localised committees were tasked with compiling lists of suitable people who were 'willing to provide hospitality of a private nature.' Those lists were then submitted to the WVS Regional HQ and passed on to the ARC who would then send copies to the Special Service Division of the US Army. The intention was that American soldiers on leave would then have the fullest available information as to the hospitality available in various parts of Northern Ireland. Furthermore, it was also decided by Brooke's committee that these hospitality lists should be available to both British and American army authorities.

Louisa Farrand
Courtesy of The American Red Cross. All Rights Reserved in all countries. 13011-001

BIOGRAPHY: LOUISA FARRAND

From the numerous American staff who served in Northern Ireland with the ARC, Louisa Farrand's wartime service is perhaps the most interesting. Born 10 December 1902 and a graduate of Cornell University, Farrand worked for the British War Relief Society before America entered the conflict. She joined the ARC and volunteered for overseas service. Farrand had arrived in Northern Ireland by May 1942 and was briefly posted to the ARC club in Londonderry ahead of her assignment to Belfast as assistant club director. She later transferred to England, and was notable for her involvement in the provision of Aeroclubs and Clubmobiles for USAAF units stationed there through 1943.

In July 1944 she became club director of Club Victoire in Cherbourg, the first ARC service club to operate in France during the Second World War. Farrand again moved on and established clubs in Le Havre and then in Belgium, where she opened three clubs over one month. One was bombed on its opening night, but still managed to be operational only an hour behind schedule, while another was forced to close after receiving a direct hit. She remained in Belgium until the conclusion of the war where she ran a staging area camp called Camp Tophat on the outskirts of Antwerp where personnel were processed for their return to the US.

In recognition of her wartime service, Farrand was awarded the US Army's Bronze Star and continued working for the ARC in its public relations department at their national HQ in Washington, DC before marrying William A Wood in 1948. In her later life she enjoyed gardening, and published a book, *Behind Those Garden Walls In Historic Savannah* in 1982. That passion for horticulture was demonstrated further when between 1983 and 1989, she attained the position of head gardener at Owens-Thomas House. Louisa Farrand passed away on 6 December 1994, aged 91, and was buried in Hillsborough, Orange County, North Carolina.

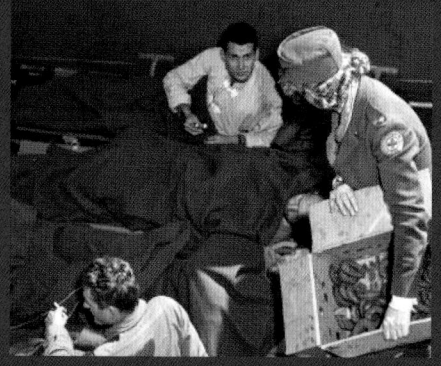

25 September 1944, Louisa Farrand serving doughnuts to wounded soldiers being evacuated by ship from France. *11278-001 Courtesy of The American Red Cross. All Rights Reserved in all countries.*
© *The American National Red Cross*

The involvement of Farrand in the scheme came to the attention of her hometown's local newspaper, *The Brewster Standard*, in November 1942. Their interest was maybe to be expected, as her father, Livingstone Farrand, was a prominent member of the community, a former Chairman of the ARC, and President of both Colorado and Cornell Universities. Under the headline 'Louisa Farrand with American Red Cross in Ireland help[s] entertain Yank troops' the *New York Sun* correspondent Ganet MacGowan, reported, 'Her idea of making leisure hours agreeable appeal to Ulster mothers,' and that Farrand was, 'Anxious that the boys overseas maintain touch with the comforts and dignities of family life.' However, by the time of the article's publication, the establishment of the hospitality committees had largely arrived too late for the benefit of American troops then stationed in Northern Ireland. It would be another year before the potential of the scheme was fully realised. As the new committees set about their tasks, some dismay became evident. One local committee perceived a lack of interest from the American commanding officer, but was unaware of the reason behind his apparent ambivalence; that officer was only too aware of the unit's impending departure and the operational reasons behind it. At the meeting of the Troop Welfare Committee on 25 November, the evolving situation was discussed, where 'it was explained that when the idea of increased facilities for the Services was first ventilated, it was anticipated that there would be a considerable number of American troops – more or less permanently – in Northern Ireland, but owing to recent events, a large number had already been dispatched to the scene of operations and more were likely to go.' As a result, the immediate work of the hospitality committees became primarily concerned with those British forces based in Northern Ireland.

Ironically, as American unit departures from Northern Ireland began, the ARC club in Belfast finally had its official dedication ceremony.

Technician 5th Grade Albert Wexler from New Jersey talking directly via a BBC short wave broadcast to Janet Barry in the US; Gene Warner from the ARC stands beside him. Janet Barry, also from New Jersey, was the overall winner in the AEF Sweetheart competition organised by the ARC in Northern Ireland. The radio broadcast was held during the Belfast club's official dedication on 10 October 1942. Janet Barry worked at the US Army Signal Corps Radio Laboratories at Camp Evans Belmar.
Author's Collection

On 10 October 1942, General Hartle, General Collins, the Duke of Abercorn, and ARC Director, Harvey Gibson were all in attendance where Hartle declared,

> '*This opening is a significant milestone of achievement, in the broad welfare program for American forces in Northern Ireland. There has been created here what is perhaps the finest and most complete Red Cross Service Club in the United Kingdom, designed and built solely for the comfort and welfare of the man in uniform. Surely it will be a great satisfaction to the families*

back home, to know that this club is here for the use of their loved ones. All who have contributed to its creation may feel justly proud. It is a pleasure and an honor to declare this ARC Service Club officially open.'

During the ceremony some light relief was provided through a direct broadcast to the US as part of an 'AEF Sweetheart' competition. Organised by Edwin Martin and christened by the local press as 'Johnny Doughboy's Rose in Ireland' competition, American military personnel were asked to submit a picture of their wives or girlfriends, from which ARC staff would pick an 'AEF Sweetheart'. Two winners were selected, one from Northern Ireland and one from the US. The local winner, Miss Brisbane Speers, an ARP volunteer from Belfast, was given the honour of the first dance with her nominee Staff Sergeant Portnov. While for the winning couple divided by the Atlantic, the prize was an opportunity to speak to each other live during the opening ceremony. The subsequent and slightly scripted address by the winning soldier, Corporal Albert Wexler to his fiancé, Janet Barry, was a highlight of the event. Official ceremony and formalities concluded, visitor books were duly signed by the guests and the evening finished with a dance with the music provided by the Ambassadors of Swing.

The provision of music and other forms of live entertainment was recognised as having a huge effect on morale, and bands such as the Lockheed Overseas Corporation's (LOC) Jive Bombers and the Navaliares from the USNOB in Londonderry provided significant incentive to attend a dance. However, a certain amount of entertainment still had to be procured and provided from existing sources. The primary organisation carrying out this role for the military in the UK was the Entertainments National Service Association (ENSA), which since its inception in 1939 had given over 200 concerts and variety shows to over 60,000 officers and men of the British forces stationed in Northern Ireland. During the spring of 1942,

The Jive Bombers, a swing band formed by members of the LOC at Langford Lodge, on stage at the Belfast ARC club early in 1943. *Courtesy of Ernie Cromie*

ENSA shows in Belfast were among the first advertised directly to US Army personnel, and by that summer ENSA had begun making a concerted effort to cater directly for US forces. During August 1942, the Londonderry ARC club began holding ENSA shows on alternate Sunday evenings, and ENSA would continue to provide a substantial portion of the entertainment for American forces throughout the war. Although welcome, it was often felt that much of the material being performed by ENSA was unfamiliar to American personnel, and its style of delivery was not always to their tastes.

To address these perceived shortcomings, the US Army's Special Service Division secured what would be the first United Services Organization (USO) tour in the ETO. Carole Landis, Martha Raye, Mitzi Mayfair, and Kay Francis arrived in the UK in November 1942 and their troupe toured for approximately six weeks, setting foot in Belfast without Mitzi Mayfair on 1 December. They performed at the Belfast ARC club followed by dates at a number of other sites across Northern Ireland. Later in the war, the ARC also ventured into the realm of providing its own entertainment through a service known as Showmobile Units. Comprised of twelve women and three men, Unit No.3 toured Northern Ireland in October 1943 and performed for US Navy and USMC personnel at Creevagh, Springtown, Lisahally, and Beechhill before a performance at USAAF Station 236 Cluntoe. Although never surpassing the activities of the USO or ENSA, nine Showmobiles were in operation throughout the UK by 1944.

Martha Raye, Carole Landis, and Kay Francis entertaining American personnel at the Belfast ARC club, 5 December 1942. *NARA*

Stars from stage and screen weren't the only significant visitors to the Belfast ARC club. In the autumn of 1942, HRH the Princess Royal (daughter of King George V and Queen Mary) viewed the club shortly after its official opening. She was received by the Duke of Abercorn and General Hartle before being presented to the staff. The Royal visitor then enjoyed afternoon tea in the club, where the white bread sandwiches were described as 'an unexpected delicacy.' More significantly for Americans, the First Lady, Eleanor Roosevelt visited on 12 November and her tour of the club concluded with the presentation of a box of Irish linen by Mildred Hughes. Mrs. Roosevelt recorded,

'The American Red Cross Club was a very nice one with a wonderful gymnasium which they also use for dancing and which must give them a really adequate floor. They have several game rooms and a very good canteen. A committee of Belfast ladies have taken an interest here and they were assembled and presented me with some pieces of Irish linen. In spite of the fact that in my hurry I hardly took time to express my appreciation of their thought, I am delighted with this gift. One of the ladies told me she was a sister of the late Mr Charles Fayerweather. It is curious in how many places one runs across people with whom there is some connection.'

With a busy schedule, Mrs Roosevelt then travelled to Londonderry where she visited the city's ARC club, noting it was 'the first one established on this side of the ocean'. The following morning after attending an Armistice Day ceremony, meeting military personnel, and viewing naval facilities, she flew to Scotland, concluding her day at the ARC club in Glasgow.

Her Royal Highness, The Princess Royal, Colonel in Chief of the Royal Corps of Signals signing the visitor's book of the ARC club in Belfast. Alice Cooke is in charge of reception and Thomas Irving looks on. 16 October 1942. *NARA*

Evident from the number of ARC clubs that Mrs Roosevelt visited during her UK tour, ARC expansion hadn't solely been confined to Northern Ireland. The club in Glasgow had opened at the beginning of August 1942 in parallel with another in Edinburgh. By 26 September there were 22 clubs in operation throughout the UK, including in Bristol, Preston, Cambridge, Birmingham, Manchester, and Liverpool. At the end of the year, the total had reached 40. However, the exodus of US personnel during Operation TORCH curtailed the need for any further immediate expansion until such time that personnel were of sufficient numbers to require additional facilities. Within Northern Ireland, ARC operations reverted to only Belfast and Londonderry while Larry C Horton from Perrysburg, Ohio, took over as Londonderry club director with assistance from Irene Starke and Barbara Wells.

After a busy Christmas period, the first half of 1943 was particularly quiet. The ARC in Northern Ireland received a commendation from Field Supervisor Roy H Hersey during a visit on 22 January. He recorded in his report that,

Soldiers and their guests at a party held in the Belfast ARC club in January 1943 commemorating the first anniversary of the arrival of American troops in Northern Ireland. The women are (left to right) Nessy Smith, Doreen Cheatly, Maureen Henderson, and Joan Greene. *NARA*

'It is my opinion that we have unusually good field service organization in Northern Ireland. While there are not so many troops there at present time, still our staff is kept fairly busy and we have a good foundation laid to take care of the contemplated expansion of the air force in this area.'

The expansion that Hersey foresaw was still some time away. It was not until the late summer of 1943 that the ARC would finally begin to provide specific services for the additional USAAF personnel arriving in Northern Ireland.

Looking west along Chichester Street, a LOC employee accompanied by an American soldier outside the Belfast ARC club. *Author's Collection*

Aeroclubs and Clubmobiles

At the request of Major General Ira C Eaker, commander of the US Eighth Air Force, one aspect of how the ARC operated in the ETO changed substantially in January 1943. The original authorisation for the ARC to operate service clubs stated that they would do so outside the boundaries of military camps, unless invited by the military authorities to do otherwise. Eaker formally extended such an invite by requesting that the ARC undertake the operation of recreational centres on all of the USAAF airfields in the British Isles.

This resulted in the ARC establishing a series of new facilities within airfield boundaries. Christened Aeroclubs, they were usually housed in a Nissen hut or similar style building and were not intended as any form of replacement for the main service clubs in towns and cities, but merely to supplement their activities by providing an informal and neutral environment to relax with coffee, snacks and other small comforts. Each Aeroclub was normally staffed by an ARC director and an ARC assistant, who would administer the club from the premises. In addition, local staff and volunteers were employed as and when needed.

The first steps to establish Aeroclubs in Northern Ireland were taken during the visit by Hersey in January 1943. Together with Field Director Elmer Quist, the two men met Brigadier General Hill, USAAF, and representatives from the US Army to explain ARC field services, their set up in Northern Ireland, and how they could benefit Hill's command. With the groundwork now laid, the USAAF activated the first of its Combat Crew

Facing page
Interior view of an ARC Clubmobile. *NARA*

Christmas Day 1943, ARC volunteers at a party held for local children at USAAF Station 236 Toome. The station's Mess Sergeant was nominated to be Santa Claus after an 'overwhelming vote in a belly contest.' In full seasonal regalia, he gave out 600 bags of candy rations donated by American personnel. Club Director Elsie Linquist is on the left.
Courtesy of Lynne Nelson

Replacement Centres (CCRC) at the airfields of Toome and Cluntoe in July and August, where in line with the new USAAF protocol, Aeroclubs were duly established. USAAF Station 236 at Toome was the first airfield to receive onsite ARC services when on 14 October 1943, its Aeroclub opened under the direction of Elsie Lindquist. The club proved to be an immediate success. During one week alone 20,000 snacks were sold and over 25 locals had been hired. Next to open was the club at USAAF Station 237 Greencastle, which came into operation on 27 October 1943 under Field Director Claude Miller. A month later Cluntoe opened on 25 November 1943, although its games room was still in the process of being completed.

At Cluntoe the ARC faced an unforeseen challenge as the allocated building was already pressed into service by USAAF personnel. It was used as an interim club of their own in which 'steaks and beer were a daily diet for all and sundry.' Henry J Cluver, then director of the Londonderry service club was assigned the delicate task of implementing redecoration and any necessary reconstruction without making the men feel wholly dispossessed. With Cluver's intervention and the premises tactfully appropriated, ARC protocols were finally implemented, and although the previously established library was retained, the serving of beer and steaks was quietly discontinued. Further expansion was planned with Aeroclubs earmarked for Maghaberry and Mullaghmore.

Through its expanding activity the ARC had also identified a need, and an inventive solution, to provide similar services to military units at more isolated locations, where operations, geography, or lack of premises had previously hindered the provision of welfare and recreational opportunities.

ARC Field Director Claude Elwood Miller was headquartered at USAAF Station 237 Greencastle, starting from 22 September 1943. In addition to overseeing activities at its Aeroclub and other ARC facilities in the area, Miller was required at the Belfast service club two days each week. His two assignments necessitated a vehicle to be procured by the ARC, with Miller then acquiring this Northern Ireland driving licence to enable him to drive it. *Author's Collection*

Francis Lux and Larry Kelley.
Courtesy of Martin Tarr

USAAF personnel, Jack Reynolds, John Knight, and Velton J O'Neal photographed outside the Aeroclub at Toome. O'Neal flew as a radio operator on board B-26 Marauder aircraft and completed 51 missions over Europe. Discharged from the military in September 1945 and upon his return to the US, he continued his pre-war career in the seafood business. The signpost that the men are standing beside first became a feature on the base during May 1944 and among others, included distances to New York, San Francisco, Berlin and Moscow. It soon became a popular location for photo opportunities, with Club Director Elsie Lindquist reporting that it was the 'Greatest morale builder yet.' *Courtesy Ted Harwood*

BIOGRAPHY: FRANCIS LUX

Employed as a teacher at Kenton, Ohio, Francis E Lux joined the ARC in June 1943 after reading about their work in a magazine. Initially arriving in England, she chose an assignment in Northern Ireland which led to a posting as Program Director at USAAF Station 236 Toome. With Club Director Elsie Lindquist, she helped establish what was the first of the ARC's Aeroclubs in Northern Ireland and organise its recreational activities. In January 1944 she took over as club director at nearby USAAF Station 238 Cluntoe, before returning to Toome that July as director until the station's closure in November 1944.

After a chance meeting with Captain Lawrence (Larry) P Kelley from the Ninth Air Force while waiting at a bus stop, it was not long before the two formally announced their engagement. A party was held on 15 April 1944 at the home of Miss F M Tate at Jubilee Cottage, Tullyroan. However, it was over a year before the couple were wed, as Francis was posted to an ARC rest and recuperation centre for USAAF personnel in Southport,

Above Autograph book belonging to Avril Shipway, with entry from Francis Lux. *Courtesy of Lynne Nelson*

Photographed during the summer of 1944, Avril Shipway with Francis Lux. Avril's father, the Rev. Percy Shipway had been organising occasional welfare activities for American forces prior to the establishment of the Aeroclub at Toome. With the arrival of the ARC, Avril became a volunteer at the Aeroclub, and Francis Lux became a friend of the family. *Courtesy of Lynne Nelson*

England, while Larry concluded his service conducting operations in Germany with the USAAF Air Disarmament Division. The couple finally married on VE Day, 8 May 1945 and a photo of their wedding at St Maire's made the cover of the *Southport Journal* newspaper.

After returning to the US, the couple raised seven children, with Larry working for NASA at their Lewis Research Center as a lawyer and contract negotiator. Francis passed away in June 2010 aged 92, while her husband Larry passed away at the age of 104 in August 2019.

During the first months of 1942, many of the American troops arriving in the UK were greeted quayside and at their camps by mobile canteens providing refreshments. Some of these vehicles and their services were provided by the WVS and the YMCA, at which point only a few comparable vehicles were operated directly by the ARC. The situation had been noticed by William Stevenson who commented that [the ARC] 'did undertake to borrow a few canteens from the WVS but they wanted to loan them to us on the basis of their women staffing them for us and wearing their uniforms.' Stevenson was not entirely happy with that arrangement and concluded, 'I think we better procure our own canteens so that we could staff them and assign them as we choose.' However, it was over a year before the ARC widely engaged in providing and staffing mobile canteen facilities similar to those operated by British agencies, but in a style and manner more tailored to American tastes and expectations.

The nature of the ARC Clubmobile concept was almost entirely defined by its name – a mobile service club. To fulfil the role within the UK, the Americans procured 40 London Passenger Transport Board, 10T10 Regal single-deck buses that had recently been withdrawn from public service. Acquisition of the vehicles initially stipulated that they were to be used

A mobile canteen serving coffee to US Army personnel at Belfast docks in May 1942. An early example of the ARC operating within Belfast port, Louisa Farrand can be seen assisting a civilian woman in providing refreshments. *Author's Collection*

as ambulances and the vehicles were configured in that role upon delivery. However, the ambulance equipment had been designed to be detachable, and was subsequently removed and put into storage before their conversion into Clubmobiles. The conversion work was carried out by Messrs Elliot of Reading with the front two-thirds of the vehicle containing all the necessary equipment for making and serving coffee and doughnuts. The rear third acted as a miniature club room, but also contained folding bunk beds for the vehicle's crew.

Each Clubmobile was staffed by three ARC female staff and carried a stock of books, magazines, writing paper, chewing gum, and cigarettes, and music was played through a phonograph to announce its arrival. From the quota of London bus Clubmobiles acquired by the ARC, one had been deployed to Northern Ireland by August 1943. But the need for additional vehicles had been anticipated and as such, requested during a visit by Northern Ireland Zone Director Herbert Kunde, to ARC HQ in London. As a result, by the end of October three more had arrived, with the four vehicles in Northern Ireland named: *New Jersey*, *Colorado*, *Oklahoma*, and *Kansas City*.

Front view of an AEC Regal 10T10 bus in use as an ARC Clubmobile in Northern Ireland. *Courtesy of the family of Corporal Technician Grade 5 Joseph F Mahoney*

Facing page
Corporal Technician Fifth Grade Joseph F Mahoney from the 8th Infantry Division standing with a coffee-filled canteen at the rear of the ARC Clubmobile named Colorado at his unit's camp in County Fermanagh during 1944. *Courtesy of the family of Corporal Technician Grade 5 Joseph F Mahoney*

The introduction of the Clubmobile service rapidly made a positive impression upon the US Army with their presence being reported as exceedingly well-received. One undisclosed division commander in Northern Ireland was so impressed by their services that he went so far as to express the desire to have them permanently attached to his division. However, that popularity naturally resulted in increased demand and Kunde noted that 'We have an urgent need for the services of four additional Clubmobiles in this area.' In what was envisaged as a temporary effort to compensate for this shortfall, the ARC arranged for the loan of a van from the Northern Ireland Area British Legion Women's Section that was christened, *Lisburn Lil*. Described by Kunde as a Studebaker (an American vehicle manufacturer) in reality it was a more diminutive British Austin. And while *Lisburn Lil* valiantly helped plug a gap in the provision of Clubmobile services, the other requested vehicles never materialised. Moreover, by the end of 1943, with troop numbers in the UK rising significantly, and both Thanksgiving and Christmas festivities to be provided, all ARC services were stretched to the full in every region where they operated.

Helen Lockwood, who served in the Belfast based Clubmobile named Kansas City, trying an alternative form of transport in Newcastle, County Down. *Author's Collection*

Expansion

Facing image Brigadier General Leroy P Collins, Commanding General of Northern Ireland Base Section (NIBS) who oversaw Services of Supply activities from the NIBS Wilmont House HQ. Through NIBS, Collins was responsible for the Special Service Division, the branch of the US Army that liaised directly with the ARC in the provision of welfare and entertainment for personnel. *Author's Collection*

Image below Requestioned at the beginning of 1944, the Pickie Hotel was used by the ARC as its service club in Bangor. In the weeks prior to D-day, naval personnel numbers were so great that to avoid overrunning the town, enlisted men were taken to Belfast while officers used the facilities in Bangor. *Author's Collection*

Between September and November 1943, more than 350,000 American troops had arrived in the UK. As the number of US Army personnel in Northern Ireland also reached new heights[1], provision for welfare services again came under consideration. The home hospitality scheme that was established in 1942 (and operated by the Northern Ireland Troop Welfare Committee) found a new advocate in General Collins, who had returned with the re-activation of NIBS during October 1943. Collins joined Brigadier Edmund Hill, USAAF and Commodore Baughman, USNOB Londonderry, as the American representatives on the committee. With the new influx of American troops, welfare aspects of their presence were discussed at length.

1. By September 1943 cumulative total of troops was 505,214 and by January 1944 the total was 1,084,752.

As troop numbers increased late in 1943, ARC worker Miss Louise Smartt from Tennessee, and volunteer Miss Josephine MacDonald from Sydney, Australia, greet newly arrived members of an anti-aircraft artillery unit in Northern Ireland with coffee and doughnuts.
12996-001 Courtesy of The American Red Cross. All Rights Reserved in all countries.

On 23 and 25 October, the American officers attended two committee meetings during which Collins expressed his view that

'We are going to do all we can to keep our officers and men out of Belfast. That is where they all want to go, but Belfast cannot hold them all. That falls in very well with this local hospitality committee program. With your help the smaller places can be made attractive enough to show our men that, after the first visit to Belfast, the country house is the better place to be.'

Collins also disclosed that it had been decided by the now Prime Minister of Northern Ireland, Basil Brooke, that this business will be carried along entirely outside of the ARC, and continued, 'The club program is being enlarged as rapidly as facilities permit. Nevertheless, the American troops are going to enjoy more the friendships which you kind of people will allow them to make, even though there are any number of Red Cross Clubs.'

Through his position as commanding officer of the service forces in the province, Collins' suggestion that visits to Belfast should be deterred may have been based simply on his insight into projected troop numbers and the proportional facilities available, rather than a desire to withhold furlough and recreation opportunities in the city. Whatever his reasons, his predictions were accurate. In December 1943, Marcia Mackie, now director of the Belfast ARC club wrote in her monthly report, 'We are operating over capacity – every facility is taxed to the utmost.' The resulting situation required the ARC to take on additional staff and local volunteers in an attempt to accommodate increasing numbers. Regardless of Collins' aspiration to keep the men out of Belfast, the draw and appeal of the city was undiminished. Over Christmas 1943, the Belfast club experienced its busiest period of the war. The rise in military personnel attending dances naturally led to an increased demand for dancing partners, with a further 60 women being issued new membership cards. This brought the total number approved as dance hostesses up to 825, with new applications still being accepted and Mackie declaring 'We can seldom have really enough girls at dances now.'

Aside from the provision of the venue, the first scheduled event relating to Christmas had little to do with the ARC. On Thursday 23 December, the LOC borrowed the ballroom to hold a party for 1,000 children. Viewed by the ARC as being extremely well planned, the children were entertained with movies, singing, music, and received presents from Santa Claus. The toys were made in four designs: Jiminy Cricket, Ferdinand the Bull, a cigar smoking bear, and a comic dog with a false moustache. Normal club activities resumed that evening with the regular dance held from 8.00 pm to 11.00 pm.

On Christmas Day, the entertainment began at 10.00 am with movies shown in the gymnasium, and at 1.00 pm soldiers from the Glee Club sang carols in the lounge.

At 2.00 pm and 4.00 pm, further movies were shown while the canteen was closed for an hour from 4.00 pm to allow for the decoration of the tables for dinner. Doors opened again at 5.00 pm when staff mustered up a group of men to sing carols with visitors joining in. From 8.00 pm to 11.00 pm a dance was held and at 11.30 pm a cabaret show began in the lounge, however the limited capacity resulted in a further cabaret show being held at 1.00 am. Events resumed on Boxing Day with another movie followed by a dance from 3.30 pm to 6.00 pm. But unlike Christmas Day, the club was declared an open house

A typical dance underway in the main hall of the Belfast ARC club. The photograph was taken during the club's official opening in October 1942. *NARA*

and the men were permitted to bring their girlfriends into the lounges where light refreshments were served. Due to rationing, it was the only time that girlfriends were permitted to be served food at the club. In the lounge, the evening concluded with square dancing, with one soldier playing the piano for three hours while jitterbugging took over one corner. On Monday 27 December, movies were run again in the morning and afternoon, followed by basketball games that evening. In her report, Marcia Mackie noted the 'tremendous efforts of all our Irish people', such as the women washing the dishes singing, and the porters giving more than their regular hours. As a thank you for their efforts, a party was held for the staff on Wednesday 29 December 'for the Irish people working in this club, and they really deserved the party for they all did a really swell job for us.'

With 1944 approaching there was little time to rest before the New Year's Eve 'big dance' which was attended by about 1,200 people. The Jive Bombers played from 8.30 pm to 12.30 am, and the majority of the women attending came in long dresses, something which was considered unusual. A floor show was held at 10.30 pm and movies were run over the weekend to take care of the large crowd's entertainment.

Similarly, other ARC clubs in Northern Ireland reported large gatherings but none exceeded those in Belfast. On the city's streets, American and British servicemen gathered at the Albert Clock to usher in the new year spontaneously and informally. As midnight approached, they joined with civilians in turning their torches on the clock dial while joining hands and dancing around the tower singing 'Auld Lang Syne'. *Stars and Stripes* reported that there were few typical New Year's Day hangovers in the ETO that Saturday morning. Although festivities had ceased by the following evening, every inch of space in the Belfast ARC club was being used for sleeping. Mackie recounted, 'I don't believe we could have packed another boy in.'

During January 1944, the intense social activity over Christmas and New Year was followed by the final and most concentrated phase of expansion for the ARC in Northern Ireland. Thirteen further premises were requisitioned by either the War Office or the Ministry of Finance and pressed into service by the ARC, mostly as day clubs. Some established locations expanded their existing facilities with 20 further ARC National Staff assigned to Northern Ireland. Possibly due to both its railway connection and proximity to attractions such as the Giant's Causeway, Portrush received particular attention beyond towns of comparable size with five premises eventually being operated by the ARC.

Two members of the USAAF outside the Slieve Donard Hotel in Newcastle, County Down. Operated as a club with dormitory accommodation, the hotel was one of 17 properties in Northern Ireland that came into ARC use on the 1 January 1944. With the vast majority of US troops deployed to County Down gone by July 1944, the hotel was returned to the War Office that August. *Courtesy of Ernie Cromie*

Featured in their brochure 'Furlough Fun', the town was described with a suggested itinerary which included:

11:40.   Arrive at the aforementioned paradise. Stoke up on mouth-watering morsels at the Trocadero or Bamford's Cafe.

2:20.   Off by tram to Dunluce Castle and the Giant's Causeway built by Finn McCool, an Irish giant of yore who intended to battle a Scottish monster. Consult the tram timetable at Portrush. Things change, you know, on this two and a half hour trip!

5:00.   Ready to return to Portrush. If not pitch a tent where you are.

6:50.   Farewell to Portrush.

Left View of Portrush in September 1944 from the balcony of the ARC service club in the requisitioned Eglinton Hotel. The ARC service club in the Savoy Cafe is also visible. *Author's Collection*

Soldiers from the 507th Parachute Infantry Regiment, 82nd Airborne Division, visiting the Giant's Causeway. *Courtesy of John McCann*

Personnel from 8th Air Force Composite Command on the Giant's Causeway Tramway. Operating between Portrush and the Giant's Causeway, the tramway was the world's first electric railway of more than 5 miles long and the first to be powered by hydroelectricity. With its Portrush terminus directly opposite the town's ARC club, the convenience and novelty of the service naturally made it a popular feature on the itinerary of many American personnel visiting the north coast on leave. *Air Force Historical Research Agency*

Return ticket for the Giant's Causeway Tramway.
Author's Collection

Furlough Fun brochure produced by the Belfast ARC club.
Author's Collection

ARC activity in Portrush centred on the Eglinton Hotel, which after requisitioning was converted into the Enlisted Men's Service Club. It opened in November 1943 and had facilities for 150 personnel. Assisted by Virginia Sutton and Hazel Kingsbury from Iowa and New York respectively, its director, Torres A Lyche from LaGrange, Illinois, was reported in a December 1943 edition of the USNOB newspaper, *Derry-NOB News*, announcing the opening of a further ARC Officer's Club. It was converted from the Bay View Hotel and cafeteria-style meals were served at the nearby Savoy Cafe. At the beginning of 1944, the ARC continued its expansion in the town adding the Station Cafe and the Orange Hall to its portfolio of properties. Activities in the latter were advertised in the *Derry-NOB* under, 'Dancing at the Orange Hall, largest dance hall in Portrush – sponsored certain nights each week by the ARC.' The venue also saw use for boxing through the ARC sports programme and achieved some notoriety when midnight mass was held there, with comments subsequently made by local MP William Lowry that antagonised the US Army and generated unwelcome publicity. In the area surrounding Portrush, the only other ARC premises were over five miles inland at Coleraine, where the ARC established one of what were known as Donut Dugouts in the Temperance Cafe on Queen Street.

Donut Dugouts were small installations that only served coffee, soft drinks, and doughnuts in areas where the number of troops and existing facilities did not justify larger establishments. Although never numerous, with less than 40 throughout the whole UK, one document from February 1944 indicates others were located in Antrim, Ballymena, Lurgan, and Portadown.

No Color Bar?

From all the ARC premises in Northern Ireland that opened at the beginning of 1944, property for two particularly unique examples was acquired on 1 January, at James Street, Belfast and Railway Street, Antrim. These were described respectively as 'Club with Dormitory accommodation for Colored Troops' and 'Day Club for Colored Troops' and were staffed by black ARC personnel. Largely segregated from their white compatriots and often employed solely in the service forces, the first black personnel from the US military arrived in the UK during the summer of 1942. Among the predominantly black units that arrived in Northern Ireland was the 28th Quartermaster Regiment. They were stationed in and around Cookstown where no ARC facility existed, yet their presence eventually warranted a visit by two of the first black ARC female staff who had arrived in the UK in October 1942. Sent on detachment from Bristol, Mary L Divers, from Handley, West Virginia, and Magnolia Latimer, from Atlanta, Georgia, were present at a dance held for the Quartermaster Regiment. However, little else is known about their visit aside from a report that they also had been taken for a ride in a pony and trap.

Black ARC staff at a dance held in Cookstown for members of the 28th Quartermaster Regiment in October 1942. Left to right are: William E Temple, ARC from Washington, DC; Mary L Divers, ARC, from Handley, West Virginia; Magnolia Latimer, ARC, from Atlanta, Georgia and First Lieutenant Mulrose, US Army Chaplain. *NARA*

The ARC had been notified that black personnel would be 'accorded the same leave and furlough privileges as other soldiers and consequently they can expect to come into their clubs.' The only apparent evidence of this happening in Northern Ireland was the use of the main hall in the Belfast service club by several basketball teams formed by black personnel. Although the US Army and ARC both desired harmonious relationships, having clubs used by both white and black personnel was still seen as potentially problematic, as was demonstrated in Newry.

The 626th Ordnance Ammunition Company had arrived in Northern Ireland on 12 January 1944, with 6 white officers and 171 black enlisted men being stationed at Drumantine School outside Newry. Aside from a weekly dance for black troops in Bessbrook, Newry was designated as the 'evening pass' centre for the troops, with 18 different units from the surrounding area also having access. For the men from the 626th, use of the town's sole ARC canteen was available up to 5.00 pm each day. After that, black personnel were restricted to the west side of the Newry Canal which divided the town and denied them access to the canteen. Although the 2nd Infantry Division was trying to assist the ARC in opening a canteen specifically for black troops in Newry, securing premises was proving difficult and in one minor incident, approximately 30 black personnel were picked up by the Military Police after inadvertently crossing from west to east.

During a subsequent enquiry carried out by XV Corps, when asked if there was segregation in Newry, the restrictions were described as the result of a mutual agreement. However, the commanding officer from the 626th stated that due to the treatment of his men, they no longer wished to visit Newry and he was granting passes for visiting Belfast instead. It's conceivable that those men then made use of the newly operational ARC club specifically for black personnel on James Street, although the only additional information as to their activity in Belfast was that the men reported that they were well treated. The James Street club was staffed by Director Earl Howard and Assistant Club Director Geneva Mercomes, both of whom were assigned to Northern Ireland on 19 January 1944. The club contained full canteen facilities, an information bureau, dormitories, a recreation room, a restroom, and was noted for having an elevator. Outside of Belfast, the only other ARC premises specifically for black personnel was the day club in Antrim that served some nearby quartermaster units. Operations there were overseen by Clarice Brooks, a former New York social worker, who had worked in Clubmobiles before her assignment to Northern Ireland. Aside from these, premises requisitioned for use by black personnel in Northern Ireland never exceeded two locations, with little information on their actual welfare activities emerging.

Although involving relatively small numbers of their staff, the provision of welfare services at American military hospitals in Northern Ireland was the first example of the ARC fulfilling their directive for the US forces. These two photos from 1944 at the US Army's 28th Station Hospital near Irvinestown were from a series taken to illustrate a typical Red Cross worker's day. That afternoon a movie was being arranged by the ARC when seemingly the equipment broke down. A projector was then borrowed from the RAF stationed nearby, with the equipment arriving courtesy of a US Army Ambulance. *12983-005 and 12983-006. Courtesy of The American Red Cross. All Rights Reserved in all countries. © The American National Red Cross 1944*

Combat Ready

Outside of a small presence in US Army hospitals, assisting in securing supplies and recreational equipment, and providing information on local matters, the ARC had until this point been largely removed from sites and camps operated directly by the US Army. But following the lead set by the USAAF in establishing clubs on its bases, the US Army followed suit. Two clubs opened in January 1944 within the camps at Mourne Park and Ballyedmond. Together with the normally expected recreational aspects, both clubs provided a more immediately accessible facility for the personnel at the camps.

The popularity and convenience of Ballyedmond resulted in its snack sales outstripping those of the three nearest service clubs combined: 87,572 snacks were sold during February and 4,500 cups of coffee were sold in one evening alone. Both clubs' locations placed them closer than ever to the realm of military operations, often serving men participating in training exercises. Whenever the clubs were notified that men would be returning from an overnight exercise, they opened at irregular hours to allow them to have coffee and sandwiches. The provision of refreshments to soldiers clad in fatigues, tired and weary after military exercises, could be seen as a precursor to the ARC's eventual operations near the battlefields of Europe.

Major General S LeRoy Irwin, Commanding General of the 5th Infantry Division viewing an artillery demonstration during March 1944 in the Mourne Mountains. Attended by all available personnel from the division, the ARC were also on hand with one of their staff visible to the right wearing an M-1 steel helmet. *Author's Collection*

Several of the organisation's own scheduled programmes were also indicative that combat operations soon lay ahead. The introduction of French language classes in clubs proved a popular addition, and discussion groups were held with exchange officers concerning military matters overseas. At Ballyedmond, Lieutenant Jaques Le Bailey spoke about his experiences as a member of the Free French underground. In Belfast, the ARC arranged for the use of the Ormeau Baths to hold combat swimming courses. These courses were first established in the US, with similar courses beginning in London in July 1943. They taught army personnel the fundamentals of swimming, how to save lives, and how to swim under battle conditions wearing battle fatigues and combat equipment. In Northern Ireland, the course was introduced during October 1943 at the requisitioned Ormeau Baths where the pool was open from 9.00 am to 9.00 pm every day, including Sunday. Courses were conducted by the ARC Athletic Department and one full week was reserved for each infantry unit. Teaching was done by water safety instructors taken from the enlisted men with an officer in charge. Overall, 1,738 men took advantage of the course. In at least one recorded instance of role reversal, the army provided training for ARC personnel. Margaret

First brought to London by the ARC in July 1943, combat swimming classes were a development of their basic swimming, lifesaving and water safety courses. Here soldiers in fatigues are learning the lifesaving 'level off' prior to 'collar carry'.
10778-055.
Courtesy of The American Red Cross.
All Rights Reserved in all countries.
© The American National Red Cross 1944

Sorenson, the Ballyedmond club director, spent a week at the US Army Driver's School after which she was considered a fully licensed US Army truck driver. She described her experience as 'becoming versed in hitching up a trailer to a 2 ½ ton truck and removing its dual-wheel.'

Naturally, the ARC still excelled in its core role of welfare provision. With troop numbers at their highest level during early 1944, the range of activities provided was more diverse than ever. A selection of programmes arranged in County Fermanagh included a turf cutting competition in Enniskillen and a shooting competition involving the Ulster Home Guard. At a more light-hearted event described by *Stars and Stripes* as a singing duel,

> 'The editor of the Enniskillen newspaper The Impartial Reporter *sang Negro Spirituals, while G.I.s retaliated with Irish Folk Songs. The whole attending audience was taught the words of 'Mairzy Doats', that all America is singing, and the gayest possible time was had by all.*'

In County Down, outdoor activities reached new proportions when the Ballyedmond club scheduled a picnic on 14 May. A convoy of eight US Army trucks left the camp at midday and called for girls in four towns with no one allowed to take part unless they had a pre-arranged date. The lunch itself consisted of potato salad, baked beans, devilled eggs, sandwiches, cakes, coffee, and pop.

For recreation, balls, bats, horseshoes, badminton sets, and fishing tackle were taken along for the 200 participants. Sorenson wrote in her report that 'several boys said to me, "I actually feel like an American again today" and "I feel like I'm living again".' ARC volunteer worker Sadie Lineker also recalled one of these events,

'We went to the Mourne Mountains and stately homes… we went on a picnic, the boys brought sandwiches with peanut butter and jelly. We couldn't figure it out, they asked "did we like peanut butter and jelly?", and we were all "how did they get jelly into a sandwich "… so all the girls said "oh we'll have jelly" to see what it was and it was jam… we all loved the peanut butter too, we thought it strange but we got used to it.'

Two interior views of the ARC day club in Warrenpoint. Personnel from the 5th Infantry Division relax as Private Romaine E Wallace from McKenzie, Tennessee, applies the finishing touches to one of two murals painted by him. Occupying a portion of the Alexandra Cafe, the club opened on 1 January 1944 and closed on 29 July 1944. ARC staff member Graham Cleaver from Plainfield, New Jersey, is standing behind the counter. *NARA*

The Sports Program

Originally the organisation of team sports for US forces within Northern Ireland was largely instigated by units or individuals, with little or no outside input or overall directive. Although a sporadic number of baseball games and even an American football game at Ravenhill rugby ground took place, these were primarily showcase or charitable events attended by curious onlookers. A more formal approach to facilitating competitive sports began after the formation of the Athletic Section of the Special Service Division in July 1942, initially with a softball league in London.

From the late summer of 1942 at sites such as Langford Lodge and those belonging to the USNOB Derry, a more diverse range of sporting activities took place. Sailors and marines from the USNOB Derry were among the first to organise themselves into a twelve-team league, playing volleyball and softball in the bases' recreation halls. But as yet, only limited interaction between the respective services had taken place. Through the departure of the 34th Infantry and 1st Armored divisions, any possibility for establishing broader participation or inter-service leagues was confined to the limited remaining US Army service forces, together with the USAAF, USMC, US Navy, and the LOC. Fortunately from the outset, the Belfast ARC club had incorporated a hall that could be adapted for several purposes including sports, enabling the club to become the focal point for a basketball league involving 21 teams that began in November 1942. Among the teams playing were the *Wolverines*, the *Nightsticks*, the *Dead Ducks*, the *Wahoo Boys*, the *Ragpickers*, the *Longshoremen*, and LOC's *Amertex* whose performances

The US Army Services of Supply, Northern Ireland basketball champions in the Belfast ARC service club, March 1943. The men are Private Guido Peluso, Sergeant Tommy Wyatt, Technician Grade 4 Leonard Baer. Back Row: Technical Sergeant Joseph P Durkin, Technician Grade 4 Owen R Poucher, Private Jessie L Noe, and Staff Sergeant James M Blalock. *NARA*

and results were greatly helped by two former university league players enabling them to take the overall tournament crown. Throughout the winter, Northern Ireland's climate contributed to sports remaining largely indoors, but a more concerted effort to provide outdoor competitive team sports began in 1943.

Photo taken during the finals of the Services of Supply Northern Ireland Basketball Championships, held in the Belfast ARC service club, 22 March 1943. *NARA*

Ravenhill, the home of Ulster Rugby that had previously been used for the solitary American football game, found more prolonged usage. Requisitioned for use by the ARC, it became the primary location for the first baseball league in Northern Ireland. The opening day's play began in fine weather on 22 May, with ceremonies including the raising of the American flag accompanied by a US Navy Construction Battalion (Seabee) band. Play was initiated when Colonel I S Dierking from the US Army threw out the first ball, with Commander Thomas Keane, United States Naval Reserve receiving. Four teams were present and the opening game saw USAAF Composite Command's *Dodgers* pitted against the *Blues* from the US Navy. Next the *Pill Rollers* from the US Navy Hospital at Creevagh, took on the *Agitators* from a US Army Quartermaster unit. In their game, the score was tied 4–4 after the sixth innings; however, the Northern Irish weather deteriorated, prompting the umpire, Sergeant Doug Gray from Washington, DC, to stop the game, much to the annoyance of those involved. But with the league now firmly established, it was only a matter of time before interest spread and the league expanded.

Two images from baseball games at Ravenhill during 1943. The top image shows the Seabees band playing while the Stars and Stripes are being raised during the inaugural game of that season, while in the photo below, Guido Peluso makes a hit for the US Navy's Blues against a USAAF team on 18 August 1943. *Author's Collection and PRONI D2334/6/12/132*

One of the most successful baseball teams was made up of the men employed by the LOC who again adopted the *Amertex* moniker previously used by the LOC basketball players. Among the other teams taking part were a newly organised USAAF team named *The Mustangs* who first played at Ravenhill on 27 June, beating the US Army's *Pelicans*, 5–3. They were joined by another baseball team named the *Air Raiders* who unsurprisingly also came from the USAAF. Perhaps more significantly, a USAAF team from England named *The Eighth Air Force Airmen* came to Northern Ireland for a brief tour beginning on 14 August at Ravenhill. In front of a crowd of more than 2,000 servicemen and civilians, Brigadier General Edmund Hill reviewed the teams while Sir Basil Brooke pitched the first ball.

Among other noteworthy games that took place at Ravenhill, a number of female ARC formed their own baseball team and named themselves *Mother Mackie's Chickens*, a clear reference to the Belfast Club Director, Marcia Mackie. They played their debut game against the *Officers' and Gentlemens' Aggregation* from 8AFCC. A slightly derisive account of their performance described Irene Boyce 'knocking a home run or something' with Mary Laverack's attendance notable 'just for being there and looking so nice at the plate.' Ultimately, although maybe unsurprisingly, previous experience prevailed and the 8AFCC team won 11–2.

Participation by women in competitive sports against male opposition was clearly a rare occurrence. Moreover, some surprise was evident when it was revealed in August 1943 that the Northern Ireland Baseball League (and indeed the wider ARC sports programme) was being managed by the aforementioned Irene Boyce. Boyce had been active in the position for two months before her contribution became a story in its own right.

The ARC female baseball team *Mother Mackie's Chickens* pictured at Ravenhill in August 1943. Marcia Mackie is third from the right, with Irene Boyce beside her and Mary Laverack behind. Note the ARC Clubmobile in the background. *Courtesy of Bunty Mackie Portig*

Despite her self-confessed ignorance of the game, she successfully arranged schedules, found umpires, refereed managers meetings, located equipment, and allegedly even settled disputes. In addition to highlighting the ARC's contribution to the sports programme, Boyce's efforts were only one instance in which the enterprise and adaptability of the largely female ARC staff became more widely recognised. At the conclusion of the baseball season at the end of summer 1943, winning teams from Northern Ireland made the journey to London to play in the ETO championships but none of them made it past the second round. Undismayed, the players dropped the curtain on the season by celebrating their achievements with a sports jamboree at the Belfast ARC club on 14 October, where more than 200 players from 14 teams attended. For the ARC and Special Services however, planning for the winter sports programme had already begun.

Portrait of Irene Boyce by Belfast artist Doris Blair. *NMNI BELUM. P67.1984* © *The Estate of Doris Violet Blair, Ulster Museum Collection*

Biography: Irene Boyce, Program Director

Born in 1913, Irene Boyce was a native of Barryton, Michigan, and typically for ARC personnel, university educated. Attaining a Bachelor of Science degree from Western State Michigan University at Kalamazoo, she subsequently became involved in social work, physical education and counselling, before becoming assistant to the athletic director then recreation director of the Ann Arbor Public Schools and Park Department. On 1 November 1942 she joined the ARC and after arriving in Belfast during January 1943, was assigned as program director at the city's service club where her previous experience was used to her advantage. Boyce's posting to Northern Ireland also resulted in her meeting her future husband William Hall, who worked for LOC at Langford Lodge. The couple were married at the Jordanstown Episcopal Church on 20 March 1944 and after the war returned to the US, living in Sioux Falls, Iowa.

Due to the influx of personnel in late 1943, the number of teams expected to participate in the new basketball league was to be double that of the previous year. Two divisions were organised: 'A' for the more highly skilled players, and 'B' for those less accomplished. Each of these was then sub divided into 'brackets'. The new basketball league officially opened its season on 25 October at the Belfast ARC club when a team of US Military Police played another from the port HQ. During the season, average spectator attendance in Belfast was approximately 300, but the league also used the gymnasiums at the USNOB Derry and Langford Lodge. LOC's previous Northern Ireland champions *Amertex* returned, but their probability of retaining their title was less than certain. Regardless, increasing troop numbers brought a swift conclusion to this league.

ARC Program Director Irene Boyce (centre) in the Grand Central Hotel, Belfast with Bebe Daniels (left) and Ann Dvorak (right) who were visiting Northern Ireland as part of a USO tour. *NARA*

A more extensive league began on 15 December when 56 teams were entered in seven divisions of eight. Among those presenting a serious challenge to the favourites, *Amertex*, were eight teams from the 5th Infantry Division and 82nd Airborne Division's *Spiders*. To enable all these teams to play, it was necessary to start the basketball games in the afternoon to make way for the evening social activities in the run up to Christmas.

Photographed in September 1943 near Rostrevor, County Down, with Captain John Manning from the Royal Army Medical Corps, Assistant Program Director Mary Laverack worked with Irene Boyce in providing recreation activities at the Belfast club. Laverack was born in 1916 in Buffalo, New York, before her family moved to Brookline, Massachusetts in 1926. She graduated from the Winsor School in Boston in 1935. Returning to the US after the war, she married in 1946 and raised a family in Sherborn. *Courtesy of Mary Sisson*

The 1943–44 season finale was again held in the Belfast ARC club and saw the 5th Infantry Division's *Ramblers*, (from the 2nd Infantry Regiment based in Newcastle) prevail over *Amertex* 20–16 in the semi-finals. They went on to play a team from the USAAF 597th Station Complement Squadron called *The Yanks*, who had finished the season with fourteen wins and three defeats, in the final. With their commanding general attending as part of the largest crowd of the year, *The Yanks* lost to *the Ramblers* 27–20 in a closely fought final.

One 'brackets' in the Class B league consisted of teams made up entirely by black personnel. These were the *Depoteers, Quintones, Globe Trotters, Pythons, Dockers, Firefighters, The Mystic Knights, Renaissance, Royal 5,* and *The Tyrone's*. Initially, games were segregated and black teams only played black teams but as the tournament progressed and teams were eliminated, segregation eventually gave way. From the twelve teams that participated in the Class B Championships held in the Belfast ARC club over the weekend of 4–5 March 1944, four comprised of black players. The first day saw the first non-segregated game when the *Royal 5* played the USAAF's *Panthers*. The final itself involved a white team, the *Rambling Wrecks* playing a black team, the *Globe Trotters* with the former winning 30–18.

The final was not the last meeting between white and black teams. By April 1944 further black teams such as *The Rams, Ballyvites, Harlemites, Hanks Hammers* and *the Bay Staters* were playing. Notably, on 2 April the USMC *Leathernecks* were defeated in Belfast 27–24 by *The Rams,* who were comprised of black players from a port unit. They were coached by Corporal Hershel Borah and their key player, Private Alfred Price, led the scoring with 12 points while three others scored 4 each. From those, Al Parks from Raleigh, North Carolina was singled out for special mention with *Stars and Stripes* reporting that he played an 'outstanding floor game for the winners'.

Bouts and a Brawl

In contrast to other sports involving the Americans, boxing had an established tradition in Northern Ireland at both an amateur and professional level. Less dependent on shipped equipment and able to utilise that which existed locally, those wishing to compete in the sport could easily find opponents in other Allied services or even civilian clubs or organisations. However, it was not until March 1943 that the ARC in Belfast arranged a competitive boxing tournament. The competition drew from all American service personnel in the province and was under the direction of one Arthur Anderson, chief instructor at the Crown Amateur Boxing Club in Belfast. As an established member of the local boxing community, Anderson was placed in charge of training that was conducted each weeknight and Saturday afternoons at the Belfast ARC club.

Seaman 2nd Class Clem Russo was one of the leading boxers from the USNOB. Russo participated in the third boxing 'smoker' to be organised by the USNOB in January 1943. The main event saw Russo compete against Paddy Harkin, a local 175 pounder of high repute. The match was described in a contemporary account as 'opening the eyes of every fight fan with Russo's rugged two-fisted attack which never let up.' *NARA*

Five boxing bouts and two wrestling matches were scheduled to take place on 22 April 1943 at the Belfast ARC club. One of the most anticipated matches was to be the light heavyweight fight between Clem Russo, a leading US Navy fighter from Philadelphia, and Cloyd Baker, a LOC technician from Los Angeles, who had fought nearly 100 amateur and professional fights. Watched by a crowd that was estimated at over 800, the expected fight failed to materialise after a Londonderry based Seabee, Carpenter's Mate 3rd Class Francis Loucka, floored the LOC favourite three times in 58 seconds. Loucka went on to fight in a tournament in London where he reached the semi-finals. Locally the sport experienced a lull in activity until it was revived through the new ARC sports schedule in December when it once again came under the supervision of Arthur Anderson.

Brigadier General Edmund Hill (right) then Commanding General of the US forces in Northern Ireland, awarding a medal to Private Joseph Domiter, USMC. Domiter had been crowned welterweight champion at the USNOB in Londonderry having won his fight against Sergeant Samuel Coggins in less than a minute. Held at the ARC club in Belfast during April 1943, the fight took place during the inaugural show of the *Stars and Stripes* Northern Ireland boxing program. Mr Frank Kammerlohr, ARC, is shown holding the microphone. *Air Force Historical Research Agency*

Divided into nine categories from flyweight through to heavyweight, the ARC used the former Rialto Ballroom at Peter's Hill, Belfast, in addition to the ARC club on Chichester Street. Attendance was encouraged through the provision of directions by streetcar (tram) or on foot, with the building referred to simply as the one with the Military Police standing outside. No tickets were deemed necessary and servicemen were permitted to bring guests. With an increase in participants, boxing matches took place within individual units' respective deployment areas and at a more diverse range of venues. For example, the 82nd Airborne Division held their preliminary rounds in the requisitioned Orange Hall in Portrush. From each of these outlying tournaments, teams then came to Belfast with their coaches, and spent several days in the ARC club to train and condition for the overall Northern Ireland Championship. In common with the previous year, boxers also travelled to London. During February, a team representing an undisclosed Northern Ireland based infantry unit fought in the main London ARC club at Rainbow Corner, but went down to a smashing defeat 6-2.

In a chance to regain their pride, a rematch was held on 18 February at the Belfast ARC club, when Private Marlon Guana came within a point of upsetting the visitors. He fought Private Charles Schnappauf, reputedly the hardest socking welterweight in the ETO, but Guana absorbed his punches without flinching. When Schnappauf was announced as the winner by one point, the home crowd of approximately 700 booed the verdict for several minutes.

The 1943-44 Northern Ireland Boxing Championship was brought to its conclusion over two nights at the beginning of April. Twenty-six fighters took part and on the final night there was a capacity crowd of over 2,000. Private Willard Martin from Pemberville, Ohio, won the heavyweight crown to roaring approval. Rivalling their match for action was a free-for-all brawl during the junior welterweight title bout between Private Jimmy Gill and Corporal Anthony Galle that involved the two not only using the ring posts to slap each other but also 'borrowing seats' from the fifth row to throw at each other.

Other notable sporting events organised by the ARC included an open golf tournament at Royal Portrush Golf Club in February and March 1944. Gunners Mate 3rd class Raymond W Malain from Detroit and Corporal Halsey Schaneen of Emerson, New Jersey overcame 135 other players to contest the final with Malain cruising to victory. The first annual 'Ulster Bicycle Derby' was also held in March 1944 on the airfield at Toome. It was watched by a crowd numbering approximately 4,000 and 10 races were held, with the four-mile main sweepstake event won by Douglas Stayton, an RAF mechanic attached to a maintenance unit at the USAAF station. Events such as these were an exception, and in the majority of ARC clubs, games such as table tennis and billiards provided the majority of informal competitive events.

During the spring of 1944, an attempt, primarily driven by LOC personnel, was made to establish a new baseball league similar to that which operated throughout 1943. Despite some initial success, the league was increasingly hampered by outgoing troop movements and military operations that depleted both participants and spectators. Furthermore, Northern Ireland's weather soon intervened, playing havoc with the schedule and forcing the cancellation of most games. As a result, interest slackened considerably, teams disbanded, and by August the rain was the ultimate victor of the 1944 season.

Facing Page
Children at a Christmas party arranged by the LOC and held in the Belfast ARC service club during December 1942. The wooden toys being held aloft were made by LOC staff in their workshops at Langford Lodge.
Courtesy of Ernie Cromie

The Stars and Stripes War Orphans Fund

From the inaugural copy of its London edition, *Stars and Stripes* included information and stories relating to and promoting ARC activities within the UK. A mutually beneficial relationship ensued from which the most enduring result of this cooperative effort must surely have been the *Stars and Stripes* War Orphans Fund. Launched in September 1942, it was a fundraising scheme for children who had lost one or both parents through wartime events. At the request of the newspaper, the ARC agreed to be responsible for both the administration of the funds

Front page of the 27 March 1943 edition of Derry-NOB News encouraging Naval personnel at the base to contribute to the *Stars and Stripes* War Orphans Fund. *Author's Collection*

collected and for all administrative expenses. In return, *Stars and Stripes* was responsible for the collection of funds and handling the publicity of the programme. With the plan officially approved by General Eisenhower, the administration was assigned to the Civilian Relief Department of the ARC which was headed by William L Gower. Its defined objectives were that the amount subscribed annually for each child was to be twenty pounds sterling over a period of five years and that enough money be raised by voluntary contributions from the American personnel to assist at least 500 war orphans throughout the UK.

Each child was to be protected from any undue publicity, with their surnames withheld from both the sponsoring unit and the press. Photographs of the child could only be requested after the selection had been confirmed and, as a further precaution, all correspondence with the family was to pass through an assigned caseworker. Additionally, there was to be no direct correspondence between the family and the administrators, or between the family and the assisting unit. The scheme was to include not only British orphans but also those from Allies domiciled in the UK. To begin the process, the first child was sponsored by Lieutenant Colonel Llewellyn from *Stars and Stripes,* while the next two children were sponsored collectively by the paper's London edition staff. Dominating the front page of the 26 September issue, under the headline, 'American Doughboy Is Their Uncle Sam', details of the first three children were published. A week later, the newspaper reported that executives of the ARC club in Londonderry had wired that they wanted 'to adopt a youngster'. A week later, an infantry unit in Northern Ireland was reported as telegraphing,

'Sure we want one-twelfth dozen or more orphans. Pick us one to be sweetheart of the regiment. Funds guaranteed to follow.' After their request, the Londonderry ARC club subsequently adopted the fourth orphan in the scheme.

The aforementioned infantry unit was the 2nd Battalion, 133rd Infantry Regiment, and they sponsored six children all from the same family.

A little girl photographed during her birthday party at Wilmont House on 1 July 1943. She was adopted by personnel from Northern Ireland District, Services of Supply through the *Stars and Stripes* War Orphans Fund. *NARA*

From their site at Langford Lodge, the American civilian employees of the LOC made the single largest donation to the fund and this resulted in the sponsorship of 16 children; more than any other unit or organisation in the whole of the UK. Championed within the company by the base's civilian chaplain, Rev. Norman E Nygaard, its beginnings were described as passing a hat to get funds for a Christmas party for the kids in Northern Ireland. As a venture that was still entirely of their own organisation, that collection amounted to £534, which was sufficient for 4,000 children to be entertained at 12 different venues.

After expenses, a sum of £200 remained from which the nucleus of a drive to raise £1,000 for the War Orphan Fund began. Base Manager Henry Ogden organised the campaign and set a modest quota for each department. The personnel from Depot Engineering donated over twice their quota and then challenged the other departments to match it. Also contributing to the drive was the LOC's *Nitwit Network* radio station, which announced that refreshments would be on the house for anyone who visited the studio and made a donation in the bucket; a few hours later the bucket was full.

A cheque for £1,632 being handed over by Henry Ogden, Manager, on behalf of LOC at Langford Lodge, to Winifred Rose, London Secretary-Treasurer of the *Stars and Stripes* War Orphans Fund. Looking on are Rev. Norman Nygaard, Chaplain for LOC and instigator of the scheme at Langford Lodge with Corporal Jacob Miller, Northern Ireland Regional Manager of *Stars and Stripes* on 6 March 1943. *Courtesy of Ernie Cromie*

When the last shilling was accounted for, the LOC estimated that they had an over-subscription of 62%. In March 1943, a visit was made to Belfast by the ARC supervisor to arrange for the selection and assignment of the children. Eight boys and eight girls were chosen from the older age range of 7-12 years and the LOC requested that only children residing in Northern Ireland be submitted. With all formalities completed Marcia Mackie assisted with the preparations for a party for the 16 children. LOC's generosity was above and beyond what was expected and their provision for a party was noted by the ARC, with a report from April 1943 drawing particular attention to it.

> 'The day was a great success: the weather was fine, the children beautifully dressed and on their best behaviour. The Lockheed men did them proud. When they arrived they were taken for rides in Jeeps, Scooters, and then in a transport plane up and down the runways, which was a real thrill. After that various types of planes were inspected and the children were allowed to sit in the cockpits and so on. A delicious lunch was served at which the children divided into four groups so that four different messes could have them as their guests. A Field Director accompanied one group for lunch, a caseworker the second, an American Red Cross Club personnel the third and a Club Director the fourth. After lunch they were each given a little box of candy and then went to a picture show which included a Pop-eye Film, a News Reel and "Dumbo". At the conclusion of the picture show Dr[sic] Nygaard of the Lockheed Overseas Corporation made a little speech and each child was called up on to the stage, presented with a little wooden suitcase with its first name painted on it, and the children were introduced to the department of the Lockheed Overseas Corporation which was sponsoring her or him. Pictures were taken and a rousing cheer given for the children.

At 4.00 pm they all adjourned to another mess hall for a right good feed of ice cream which everyone thoroughly enjoyed. They then went back and each child's case was filled with candy and cookies and other goodies for them to take home to their families. At 5.15 pm they all set off on the return journey-each child was deposited home tired but thoroughly happy.'

Although unmatched in scale, the LOC wasn't alone in its charitable contributions. The 6 March 1943 edition of *Derry-NOB News* marked the beginning of the USNOB's fund-raising drive when it announced a base war orphan adoption goal of 25 children. Starting with $2 per man from hut 15 ($20), by 27 March the fund was reported as having reached $132.40. However, the base's target to sponsor 25 children was never realised, with only one child being adopted with the additional money submitted to the scheme's general funds.

Certificate belonging to a child who was sponsored in November 1943 by HQ 8AFCC at Kircassock House through the *Stars and Stripes* War Orphans Fund. *Air Force Historical Research Agency*

By July 1943, 46 children from Northern Ireland were sponsored within a UK total of 231. Notably, towards the end of the year members of the 818th Tank Destroyer Battalion stationed at Killymoon Castle adopted four children with their £402 contribution. Their donation was reported as one of the largest made by a unit of that size. Other units in the country who sponsored children included the HQ of 8AFCC at Kirkcassock House, 5th Airdrome Squadron HQ at Toome, 544th Quartermaster Service Battalion, and Western Base Section Northern Ireland District. But despite the subsequent troop arrivals and surge in personnel numbers in the latter half of 1943, only a further five children from Northern Ireland were adopted into the scheme.

Children sponsored by the *Stars and Stripes* War Orphans Fund on a USAAF C-47 aircraft at Langford Lodge. *NARA*

That said, the fund's overall intended goal of £50,000 and 500 orphans was successfully reached by 26 Feb 1944. Within 18 months £45,000 ($180,000) had been raised leading to the initial target being increased from £50,000 to £100,000. At the end of 1945, in line with the cessation of ARC activity in the UK, the *Stars and Stripes* War Orphans Fund was closed. Responsibility for the administration of the remaining funds was put in the hands of those local agencies that had assisted and in January 1946 the fund programme was formally wound up. Total contributions amounted to $377,196.85 with expenditures of $181.838.55, leaving a balance of $195,358.30 raised and most importantly, an immeasurable legacy for those children who were sponsored.

Facing page
VE Day parade passing Belfast City Hall, May 1945.
Courtesy of Bonar Holmes

Final Days

As the American military units in Northern Ireland were successively withdrawn, the requirement for ARC clubs began to diminish. Although one Aeroclub at Langford Lodge went against the trend and opened on 25 May 1944, conversely, the Aeroclub at Mullaghmore closed permanently on Easter Sunday 1944 having only opened ten weeks earlier. Similarly, the Orange Hall in Cookstown that had been employed as a day club was returned to the Government's requisitioning department in June and throughout July, clubs in Armagh, Ballymena, Lurgan, Newry, Omagh, and Warrenpoint all ceased operations. In a sign of the changing times, classes were held in the Belfast and Londonderry ARC clubs for women who had married American personnel. The programme was intended to familiarise the wives of American personnel who served in Northern Ireland with aspects of American life in anticipation of them moving to the US. Organised by Marcia Mackie, the last of ten classes in Belfast was a question-and-answer session with

Wives and children of US Navy personnel stationed in Londonderry, arriving in New York at the beginning of September 1944. *Author's Collection*

the American Consul General, Quincy Roberts. In addition, a leaflet titled *Fashion Do's and Don'ts for American Wives* was also produced.

The timing of the leaflet and classes was pertinent. The USNOB Londonderry was in the process of being decommissioned, and a number of its personnel returned to the US on board the SS *Marine Raven*. In what was the first example of war brides leaving Northern Ireland for the US in sizeable numbers, approximately 70 wives of US Navy and USMC personnel boarded the ship at Lisahally, where ARC staff on the quayside distributed gifts of chocolates and cigarettes. The departures on the *Marine Raven*

Group of personnel belonging to the USAAF and stationed at Maghaberry photographed at Fisherwick Place, Belfast and on their way to the Belfast ARC club.
Courtesy of Jon Maguire

occurred less than two weeks after what was arguably the last high-profile event on the entertainments programme provided at the ARC club in Belfast; one which no account of American forces entertainment would be complete without.

Glenn Miller and his orchestra arrived in the UK in June 1944 where they performed for a series of radio broadcasts before embarking on a tour playing mostly at air bases. On 13 August, Miller and his orchestra (minus the string section) landed at Langford Lodge in two C-47 aircraft. They promptly loaded their equipment onto trucks for the journey to the Belfast ARC service club, where it was reported that Miller's orchestra performed fifty-five minutes of swing in the slickest and most up-to-date manner that was enjoyed by an audience of approximately 1,200. Demand for places was high and the only civilians present were ARC volunteers. Sadie Lineker recalled that *'Everybody crowded around the stage… we were dancing around the back of the crowd.'* Possibly due to a substantially male audience, local papers observed few others bothered to dance. Those in attendance were content in simply watching the band with some doing so whilst sat on the floor. At the conclusion of the concert, Miller and his orchestra returned to Langford Lodge where after dinner they played to a capacity crowd in the base's theatre, the Proj-Ma-Hall.

As the need for ARC services continued to diminish, the ARC Officers' club occupying the Union Hotel in Belfast was decommissioned in September 1944. By 12 October, more premises had permanently closed leaving only the Belfast and Londonderry clubs active at the end of 1944, both of which had already begun to shed their surplus dormitory and office sub-sites. The two clubs continued to provide services into 1945, primarily for the remaining USAAF units, US Army and US Navy personnel in the ports, and the small number on leave or furlough. But with limited attendance and decreasing utilisation, notable events were few and far between.

Nonetheless, dances continued and as the war in Europe ended, one was held on VE Day during celebrations in Belfast, although possibly more people were dancing in the streets. Finding another outlet for their talents, the club's adaptable volunteers knitted 120 jumpers and sweaters for orphans in continental Europe. A prize was offered for the greatest number of garments knitted and was won by Mrs Peggy Harris from Malone Park, Belfast, who turned out 18 items. A year after D-Day, the Belfast club quietly commemorated its third anniversary shortly after which, for her efforts as club director and promotion of American relations, Marcia Mackie was awarded the Officer of the British Empire (OBE) in the King's Birthday Honours. The following month the completion of US Army operations in Northern Ireland was marked in a ceremony at the Belfast ARC club on Monday 6 August, during which Langford Lodge was formally returned to the RAF. Lieutenant General John CH Lee was originally scheduled to speak on behalf of the American ground forces but his attendance

The ARC service club at Waterloo Place, Londonderry. The horses and carts are providing sightseeing hay rides for American military personnel and their female companions. A recreational activity that the ARC was still providing in 1945. *NARA*

was cancelled when he was involved in a minor accident. Luckily an eminently suitable replacement was found in Major General Walter M Robertson, Officer Commanding XV Corps, who had previously been stationed in Northern Ireland in command of the 2nd Infantry Division. Those present, included Air Commodore A.R. Churchman, representing the RAF, Brigadier General JH Houghton, commanding HQ Base Air Depot area Air Service Command United States Strategic Air Forces, Brigadier General Edmund Hill, Marcia Mackie, and representatives from the Northern Ireland Government. Robertson read a message from General Lee, saying,

> *'May this partnership ever endure and may we Americans prove not unworthy of your trust in us first as guests and now as brothers in freedom under the fatherhood of God.'*

Activity in the Belfast club continued to wind down and by the middle of October, many of the furnishings were being auctioned off. Similarly in Londonderry, the Northern Counties Hotel that hosted the ARC club announced that their public bar was open for business in early November. However, it is not known when the ARC ceased operations.

Brigadier General Houghton speaking at a dinner in the Belfast ARC club, before the formal ceremony when Langford Lodge was handed over from the USAAF to the RAF. Seated left to right are Brigadier General E F Koening, Marcia Mackie, Major General WM Robertson, and Sir Basil Brooke.
Courtesy of Bunty Mackie Portig

Eventually, towards the end of November, Marcia Mackie informed the government press officer at Stormont that the ARC was officially leaving Northern Ireland. The contribution made by the ARC to the welfare of US servicemen was a hugely important and largely overlooked aspect of American military life carried out by a comparatively small number of personnel. In March 1944, only 908 American workers were recorded as being employed at 170 premises across the UK. Exactly what number was employed in Northern Ireland is unknown, but the number is likely to be no more than 150. Nevertheless, as a small snapshot of their activity during the week between 26 March and 1 April 1944, the combined clubs in Northern Ireland (excluding camps and Aeroclubs) served 68,544 snacks, 17,997 main meals and provided 10,358 beds alongside their normal selection of dances, shows, and sporting activities.

But statistics alone provide little appreciation of the activities, atmosphere, environment, or empathy encountered by all those who passed through the doors or worked within their walls. Margaret Sorenson described her time in Northern Ireland as 'without doubt, the most satisfying experience I've ever been privileged to enjoy'. In her final report from Mullaghmore Aeroclub, its director Ruth Elizabeth Smersh concluded, 'When the boys came to say goodbye there were not many dry eyes, as they were my dearest friends, and we had so many fond and happy memories. Some day we will all meet again and talk over our days at Mullaghmore in North Ireland.'

Appendix 1
Locations of the ARC in Northern Ireland

Antrim
- Presbyterian Hall,
- Orange Hall, Railway Street – Day Club for black troops

Armagh
- 25 Dobbin Street, McKenna's Hall (Billiard Saloon – Day Club 1/1/44
- 2a Dobbin Street, Commission Agents Office – Extension to club used as games room

Ballymena
- Masonic Hall (Ground Floor) – Day Club 1/1/44
- Ex-NAAFI, Ballymoney Road

Bangor
- Pickie Hotel, Mount Royal – Club with dormitory accommodation

Belfast
- 1 Adelaide Street, American Consulate – Dormitory accommodation
- 2 Adelaide Street, Henry Matier & Co Ltd – Dormitory accommodation
- 33-38 Chichester Street, Plaza Ballroom – Service club
- 22-23 College Square East, Kensington Hotel - Additional accommodation for officers' club
- 6-7 Donegall Square South, Union Hotel – officers' club
- Fitzroy Avenue, 9th Old boys Association Sports Hall, – Production and distribution of doughnuts
- 26 Howard Street – Zone Directors Office (from October 1943)
- 31-33 Gloucester Street – Dormitory accommodation
- 14 James Street South – Club with dormitory for black troops (from 1944)
- 33-35 Linenhall Street, BBC Sports Club premises – Dormitory accommodation
- 1-3 May Street, Henry Matier & Co Ltd – Dormitory accommodation
- 18 Ormeau Avenue, Swimming baths Patterson's Place, Imperial House- Store for Clubmobile foodstuffs
- Ravenhill Rugby Ground – Sports events

Castledawson
- Part of Hillhead House and shop – Accommodation for Clubmobile purposes
- NAAFI Canteen Building
- Ex NAAFI Canteen/St Patrick's Hall – Day Club

Cookstown
- Orange Hall – Day Club

Downpatrick
- Premises used during 1942 but not requisitioned

Enniskillen
- 11 Church Street

Kilkeel
- Presbyterian Church Hall

Londonderry
- Northern Counties Hotel, 20 Waterloo Place – Club with dormitory accommodation
- 3 Strand Road, Annex to 20 Waterloo Place – Ancillary dormitories
- 112 Strand Road, Barrel Factory – Recreation centre

Lurgan
- Premises in Malcolm's Factory, Queen Street

Newcastle
- Slieve Donard Hotel – Club with dormitory accommodation

Newry
- 81 Hill Street, Young Men's Christian Institution – Day Club
- 22 Water Street, Store

Omagh
- Royal Arms Hotel – Club with dormitory accommodation
- County Courthouse - Accommodation for dances

Portadown
- Brown's Shop, Bridge Street – Ancillary dormitory
- Plaza Dance Hall, Bridge Street – Day Club

Portrush
- West Bay View Hotel – Officer's Club
- Eglinton Hotel – Enlisted Men's Club
- Orange Hall – Extension to club for Enlisted Men
- Savoy Cafe – Extension to club for Enlisted Men
- Station Cafe – Extension to service club

Warrenpoint
- Portion of Alexandra Cafe – Day Club
- 36 Church Street, One room on ground floor

Clubs at US Army Camps
- Ballyedmond
- Mourne Park

Field Offices at US Army Camps
- Armagh
- Ballykinlar
- Cookstown
- Crossgar
- Enniskillen
- Londonderry
- Irvinestown
- Kilwaughter
- Holywood

Hospitals
- 10th Station Hospital, Belfast (Musgrave)
- 28th Station Hospital, Irvinestown
- 79th General Hospital, Waringfield (Moira)
- USNOB Hospital, Crevagh

Donut Dugouts
- Antrim, Orange Hall
- Ballymena, Masonic Hall
- 344 Antrim Road, Belfast (Joint facility for 7th Port with Special Services and Chaplain)
- Coleraine, Temperance Cafe
- Lurgan, NAAFI Building, Malcolm's Factory, Queen St
- Portadown, Plaza Dance Hall, Bridge Street

Appendix 2
Known ARC Staff Who Served in Northern Ireland (Zone 4)

By no means comprehensive, this list names some of those who served in ARC facilities throughout Northern Ireland. Often personnel were reassigned to a different role or location and in that respect, some information may be open to interpretation. The list excludes American nationals living in Northern Ireland and local civilians who became staff or volunteered for the ARC.

As an example of their numbers the following statistic circa November 1944 is provided:
- Belfast – 190 paid staff and 210 volunteers
- Londonderry – 14 paid staff and 87 volunteers
- Portrush – 33 paid staff and 31 volunteers

For Clubmobile and Aeroclub staff please see Appendix 3.

Staff
- Adcock, Edyth E – Staff Assistant
- Anderson, Mary – Belfast
- Barrett, Dorothy – Recreation Officer, 79th General Hospital
- Bigsby, Zone – Catering Manager, 10th Station Hospital
- Block, Leonard – Cookstown
- Bodeman, George – Zone Executive
- Bogue, Elizabeth – Director Officer's Club, Belfast
- Bolger, Mary S – Assistant Program Director, Bangor
- Boyce, Irene – Program Director, Belfast
- Boyt, Mr – Assigned 82nd Airborne
- Breakstone, Kay – Program Director, Portadown
- Brooks, Clarice – Staff Assistant
- Bozman, Miss – Social Worker, 79th Station Hospital
- Buckingham, Alice – Staff Assistant, Belfast
- Bushyeager, George – Assistant Field Director (Assigned 8th Infantry Division)
- Cappio, Alfred P – Director, Londonderry
- Cantrell, Helen – Administrative Secretary, Londonderry
- Carroll, Mr – XV Corps HQ
- Chater, Harry G – Zone Director
- Clarke, Lucille – Assistant Program Director, Lurgan
- Cleaver, Graham – Director, Warrenpoint
- Cluver, Henry J – Director, Londonderry
- Cook, Alberta – Belfast
- Coss, Miss – 28th Station Hospital
- Couderc, Marie – 10th Station Hospital
- Davies, Elsie – Medical Social Worker, 10th Station Hospital
- Derr, Sylvia – Administrative Secretary, Londonderry
- Disoway, John S – Regional Field Director
- Faris, Dorothy – Assistant Program Director, Belfast
- Farrand, Louisa – Assistant Director, Londonderry, Belfast
- Fischer, Grace – Assistant Club Director, Londonderry
- Frederick, Miss H – Staff Assistant
- Garrison, Richard – Assistant Field Director
- Gillespie, Margaret – Program Assistant
- Goodell, Frank R – Director, Londonderry
- Hagarty, Louise – Assistant Program Director
- Hall, Marian
- Harries, Alfred, Assistant Field Director – Assigned 2nd Infantry Division
- Hazlett, Effie H – Assistant Program Director

- Healey, Joseph R – Director, Londonderry
- Hersey, Roy H – Deputy Director
- Holtman, Kathryn A – Director, Mourne Park
- Horne, Monica
- Horton, Lawrence C – Director, Londonderry
- Howard, Earl - Club Director, Belfast (James Street)
- Irving, Thomas W – Recreation Director
- James, Myrle – Assistant Program Director, Ballymena
- Jones, Nancy – Belfast
- Jankowski, Frank - Field Director – Assigned 8th Infantry Division
- Kammerlohr, Frank – Program Director, Belfast
- Karas, Elsie, Assistant Program Director, Newry
- Kingsbury, Hazel – Portrush
- Kohler, Elena A – Assistant Club Director, Londonderry
- Kunde, Herbert E – Zone Director – Field Service Laverack, Mary – Assistant Program Director, Belfast
- Latimer, Sue – Lurgan
- Lowe, Miss – Assistant Club Director, Londonderry
- Lund, Herbert – Assigned 8th Infantry Division
- Lyche, Torres A – Director, Portrush
- Mahler, Mortimer – Field Director, Newcastle – Assigned 5th Infantry Division
- Martin, John - Public Relations Officer
- Martin, Thomas – Assistant Field Director
- McHale, Thomas Ford – Field Director
- McMullin, Miss – Assistant Field Director
- Mercomes, Geneva – Assistant Club Director
- Miller, Claude – Assistant Field Director
- Mott, Jones Nancy – Medical Social Worker, 10th Station Hospital
- Napier, Jean – Assistant Field Director, 10th Station Hospital
- North, Edna – Assistant Programme Director, Londonderry
- Olfe, Ernest – Program Director, Londonderry, Acting Director Portadown
- Orlousky, Philip – Assistant Field Director – Assigned 8th Infantry Division
- Payson, Mary – Assistant Program Director
- Priest, Elinor – Recreation Officer, 79th Station Hospital
- Quist, Elmer – Field Director
- Reasoner, Allen – Field Director – Assigned 5th Infantry Division
- Reynolds, Holly – Program Director, Warrenpoint
- Riegle, Robert – Director, Enniskillen
- Rice, Mary Anderson – Assistant Club Director, Bangor
- Ratcliffe, Harry – Omagh, Portrush
- Riggle, Robert – Director, Enniskillen
- Sauter, Raymond – Field Director, Armagh – Assigned 2nd Infantry Division
- Schmitt, Robert L – Field Director, Belfast
- Sefton, Marjorie – Director, Enniskillen, Armagh
- Shanahan, Eleanor – Assistant Program Director
- Shirley, Ruth – Program Director, Enniskillen
- Slocum, Jean – Assistant Director, Bangor
- Smith, Malcolm – Zone Supervisor
- Sorenson, Margaret – Director, Ballyedmond
- Speller, Miss B – Coleraine
- Spalter, Bessie – Director, Newry
- Spaulding, Miriam – 10th Station Hospital
- Starke, Irene – Assistant Program Director, Londonderry
- Stein, Marjorie – Secretary, Belfast
- Stevenson, Patricia – Secretary, Belfast
- Sutton, Virginia – Portrush
- Stone, Grace V – Assistant Program Director
- Talbot, Miss – 28th Station Hospital
- Tomassi, Mr – Zone Director, Belfast
- Trustler, Mr V – Club Director

- Varhol, Mr J G – Downpatrick
- Weir, George – Club Director
- Weller, Ruth – Secretary, 79th Station Hospital
- Wells, Barbara – Assistant Club Director, Londonderry
- Zack, Jacob – Director, Castledawson

APPENDIX 3
Aeroclubs and Clubmobiles: Sites, Vehicles and Personnel

Aeroclubs at USAAF Stations
- Station 236 Toome: Elsie Kelley Lindquist, Club Director; Francis E Lux, Programme Director
- Station 237 Greencastle: Alice Gould, Helen Bretzfelder, Gwen Nash McWilliams
- Station 238 Cluntoe: Henry Cluver, Marion G Connolly, Miss Dorothy Dresser, Francis E Lux, Ragnar Hals
- Station 239 Maghaberry: Carol Lee Davis, Francis E Lux
- Station 240 Mullaghmore: Ruth Elizabeth Smersh
- Station 597 Langford Lodge: Staff unknown

Clubmobiles
- Supervisor: Eve Christensen
  Clubmobiles. Vehicle Name, Original Serial, ARC Serial, Location.

OKLAHOMA: Serial T659, X201025:
Based in Armagh Crew No. 1: Louise Smart, Virginia Roberts, Marie Riversi, Elizabeth Harris

KANSAS CITY: Serial T668, X201113.
Based in Belfast (Previously at Barrow-in-Furness)
Crew No. 2: Fanniebelle Allen, Helen Lockwood, Barbara Gommere

COLORADO: Serial T633, X201034.
Based in Newry (Previously at Tidworth)
Crew No. 3: Jerri Ford, Dorothy Hood, Dorothy Kurtz, Margaret Lunn

NEW JERSEY: Serial T646, X201013.
Based in Rostrevor (Previously at Cheltenham)
Crew No. 4: Janet Hopkins, Jeanette Miller, Kay Mackay, Margaret Jane Paul

LISBURN LIL: (Serials unknown).
Based Rostrevor.
Employed Crew No. 4

Sources/Bibliography
Primary Sources
National Archives and Records Administration
- RG181: Naval Districts and Shore Establishments 1784–1996. 181.6.5 Records of the Londonderry NOB
- RG200: Records of the American National Red Cross 1935–1946. 900.08 American Red Cross overseas Emergency Relief Program
- RG200: Records of the American National Red Cross 1935-1946. 900.118 ETO Club Department Reports
- RG200: Records of the American National Red Cross 1935-1946, ETO 900.11/6121 Great Britain Camp Clubs
- RG200: Records of the American National Red Cross 1935-1946, ETO 900.11/6161 AAF Station Aeroclubs
- RG338: Records of U.S. Army Operational, Tactical, and Support Organizations (World War II and Thereafter) IG Section: Racial Disturbance at Newry
- RG407: Records of the Adjutant General's Office, WWII Operations Reports 1940–48, 5th Infantry Division
- RG498: Records of Headquarters, European Theater of Operations, United States Army (World War II) 538, American Red Cross, Historical Summaries, Reports, Monographs
- RG498: Records of Headquarters, European Theater of Operations, United States Army (World War II) 20A & 20B, American Red Cross

Public Record Office Northern Ireland
- CAB/9/CD/136: 1939-1943 - Prime Minister's Statements in House of Commons
- CAB/9/CD/225/19: Welfare Social Centres
- D3004/D/33: 1942 – Diary of Sir Basil Brooke
- D2086/AA/4: 1938-1952 – Minute Book of the Belfast Council of Social Welfare
- FIN/17/1P/23/2: 1942-1945 – War Records American Forces

Air Force Historical Research Agency
- IRISNUM 0225567: 0008 Air Force Composite Command
- IRISNUM 00003445: DEPOT/0403/AIR, Langford Lodge

Library of Congress
- Frances E. Lux Kelley Collection (AFC/2001/001/18263), Veterans History Project, American Folklife Center

The National Archives
- T 272/103: American Red Cross Occupations Northern Ireland

National Museums Northern Ireland
- *Stars and Stripes*, Northern Ireland Edition, 1943–1944

The Royal Voluntary Service Archive & Heritage Collection
- WRVSA&HC/WRVS/HQ/PUB/BUL/BUL-1941–02 – WVS Bulletin No.16 February 1941

Other Period Publications
- *Stars and Stripes*, London Edition, 1942–1944 Furlough Fun, American Red Cross Brochure, Northern Ireland
- Derry-NOB, Newspaper of the USNOB Londonderry
- LIFE Magazine 24 Jun 1940, US Guide to Allied Aid (P-78 List of agencies}
- *Brewster Standard*, 5 November 1942
- *Belfast Telegraph*
- *Belfast Newsletter*
- *Londonderry Sentinel*

Contemporary Publications
- George Buchanan Fife, *How the American Red Cross met the American Army in Great Britain, the Gateway to France* (Macmillan, New York, 1920)
- George Korson Coward-McCann, At His Side: *The Story of the American Red Cross Overseas in World War II* (INC. New York, 1945)
- Marcus Patton, *Central Belfast* in 'Historical Gazetteer' (UAHS,1993)
- Chris Way, *Glenn Miller* in Britain Then and Now in 'After The Battle' (1996)
- Leanne McCormick, *Regulating Sexuality* (Manchester University Press, 2009)
- Les Wilson, *The Drowned and the Saved: When War Came to The Hebrides*, (Birlinn, 2018)

Internet Sources
https://www.fold3.com
https://www.loc.gov/
https://www.findmypast.ie
https://erpapers.columbian.gwu.edu/my-day
https://www.redcross.org/content/dam/redcross/National/history-wwii.pdf
https://digicom.bpl